First printing September 2012
Cover by Working Design
Printed and bound in Canada by Marquis Printing
A co-publication of
RED Publishing
2736 Cambridge Street
Vancouver, British Columbia V5K 1L7 and
Fernwood Publishing
32 Oceanvista Lane, Black Point, Nova Scotia, B0J 1B0
and 748 Broadway Avenue, Winnipeg, Manitoba, R3G 0X3
www.fernwoodpublishing.ca

  Canadian Patrimoine NOVA SCOTIA **Manitoba**
Heritage canadien

Fernwood Publishing Company Limited gratefully acknowledges the financial
support of the Government of Canada through the Canada Book Fund and the
Canada Council for the Arts, the Nova Scotia Department of Communities,
Culture and Heritage, the Manitoba Department of Culture, Heritage and Tourism
under the Manitoba Publishers Marketing Assistance Program and the Province of
Manitoba, through the Book Publishing Tax Credit, for our publishing program.

Library and Archives Canada Cataloguing in Publication
Engler, Yves, 1979-
The ugly Canadian : Stephen Harper's foreign policy / Yves Engler.
Includes bibliographical references.
ISBN 978-1-55266-530-5

1. Canada--Foreign relations--21st century. 2. Harper, Stephen, 1959-. I.
Title.

FC242.E538 2012 **327.71** **C2012-903163-1**

Contents

Timeline of Stephen Harper's Senior Cabinet Ministers

Foreign Minister

January 2006 - August 2007 Peter MacKay
August 2007 - May 2008 Maxime Bernier
May 2008 – October 2008 David Emerson
October 2008 - June 2011 Lawrence Cannon
June 2011 – Today John Baird

Defence Minister

January 2006 - August 2007 Gordon O'Connor
August 2007 – Today Peter MacKay

Trade Minister

January 2006 – October 2008 David Emerson
October 2008 – May 2011 Stockwell Day
May 2011– Today Ed Fast

Introduction

> *"Since becoming prime minister – the thing that's probably struck me the most in terms of my previous expectations … is not just how important foreign affairs/foreign relations is, but in fact that it's become almost everything."*
>
> — Stephen Harper June 2011

While millions disagree with Stephen Harper and his Conservative Party's domestic agenda, fewer Canadians are aware of his government's destructive foreign policy. Many of us only pay close attention to matters that directly affect us, or our families. So, when the Conservatives make it harder to collect employment insurance or raise the old age pension age, people notice because it affects them, or someone they know. When a Conservative MP introduces a private members bill to restrict a woman's right to choose an abortion, media outlets across the country report on it and pundits produce reams of analysis, much of it critical. But, when our government encourages a coup in Honduras or mining legislation to benefit Canadian companies over indigenous communities in Peru, there is little critical reporting in the dominant media. This is because the only direct Canadian self-interest tends to be that of the companies trying to profit from the situation. Investors put pressure on the government to promote their self-interest while few, if any, Canadians have a direct stake in defending Honduran democracy or the rights of poor villagers in a remote corner of Peru.

The purpose of this book is to shed some light on the Harper government's international policies. Understanding what

is being done in our name is the first step to motivating Canadians to care about foreign policy. Only when enough of us care is there a possibility of developing a counterweight to the narrow self-interests of corporations and wealth holders. Only if Canadians of good will and social conscience act together to demand a foreign policy based on solidarity and mutual support will there be any possibility of achieving that goal. Only if we build a sense of solidarity between Canadians and ordinary people around the world will we have a chance of making foreign policy a significant issue in the next election. If we do nothing the status quo as outlined here will continue.

This book is about the Harper-led Conservative government's militaristic and corporate-oriented foreign policy. It documents the sordid story of this country's sabotage of international environmental efforts, of a government in bed with tar sands producers and a mining industry widely criticized for abuses. The book also details some case studies such as the Conservatives' opposition to the "Arab Spring" democracy movement and backing for repressive Middle East monarchies as well as Canada's extensive military campaign in Libya. It explores Harper's far-reaching support for a right-wing Israeli government and backing of aggression in Iran, Lebanon and Somalia. Finally, the book delves into the Conservatives' militarism, lying about Afghanistan, indifference to post-earthquake Haitian suffering and opposition to social transformation in Latin America.

These policies spurred an unprecedented international backlash against Canadian foreign policy, culminating in a stunning rebuke when the Harper government lost its bid for a UN Security Council seat in October 2010. Since Harper's first minority government in 2006, the Conservatives have been offside

from the world community on a host of issues. For example, they were repeatedly criticized for sabotaging international efforts to improve health and environmental standards; the BRICS nations (Brazil, Russia, India, China and South Africa) jointly criticized Canada's withdrawal from the Kyoto Protocol; some European Union MPs publicly complained about the Conservatives' aggressive lobbying on behalf of tar sands producers; many countries have opposed Ottawa's unflinching support of Israeli aggression; the Congolese government denounced Canada's bid to delay its debt forgiveness. Ottawa was also offside from almost the entire hemisphere over its tacit support for a military coup in Honduras and angered the Venezuelan government by meddling in that country's political affairs. In 2010 Canada (along with the US) was excluded from the newly created Community of Latin American and Caribbean States.

The anger at Canada has not been confined to diplomats and government ministers. At the grassroots level some Afghan civilians said they wanted to "kill" Canadians while Somali militants called for attacks inside this country and CSIS feared that Ottawa's actions in Lebanon could see Canada targeted. In Haiti protestors regularly criticize Canadian "imperialism" and dozens of communities across the globe are in conflict with Canadian mining companies. But this international opposition has failed to significantly alter the government's course. The Conservatives simply don't care what the rest of the world thinks. In fact, their political godfathers celebrate international hostility. To a large extent the Conservatives take their foreign policy cues from the right wing of the US Republican Party. Author Andrew Nikiforuk argues: "Republican religious tribalism is now Ottawa's worldview." Clearly, the Conservatives are inspired by individuals

such as Sarah Palin ("global warming studies … [are] a bunch of snake oil science"), Newt Gingrich ("we have invented the Palestinian people") and John McCain ("Bomb, Bomb, Bomb, Bomb, Bomb Iran"). Sounding much like Palin, Gingrich and McCain, as opposition leader, Harper repeatedly criticized Prime Minister Jean Chrétien for not fully supporting George W. Bush's 2003 invasion of Iraq.

The Conservatives have also taken an increasingly aggressive tone against the UN, a longtime punching bag of the US right. During the third UN anti-racism conference in September 2011 immigration minister Jason Kenney helped set up a counter conference in New York. (Sort of like when the anti-corporate globalization movement organizes counter summits, but in this case the organizer was a sitting cabinet minister.) The only government minister to participate, Kenney joined with former right-wing Republican presidential candidate Mike Huckabee and George W. Bush's ambassador to the UN, John Bolton, who once said "[the UN] Secretariat Building in New York has 38 stories. If you lost ten stories today, it wouldn't make a bit of difference." In June 2012 Conservative MP Larry Miller called for Canada to withdraw from the UN.

More than six years of Stephen Harper as prime minister has emboldened the most right wing elements of the Conservative Party. In fact, foreign policy is the one arena where the neoconservative leaders of the Conservative Party allow their true colours to be on display. They know that most Canadians disagree with their neoconservative, pro-US empire politics. But they also know that few of us pay much attention to what happens outside this country's borders. The goal of this book is to be a small spark in lighting a fire of interest in Canadian foreign policy.

Note on sources

Most of the information in this book is from government websites and newspapers such as the *Toronto Star*, *Globe and Mail*, *Ottawa Citizen*, *National Post*, *La Presse* and *Le Devoir*. Other sources include more specialized publications like *Embassy* and the *Canadian Jewish News* as well as a wide selection of the international press. Some of the information also comes from activist groups such as Mining Watch and the Coalition to Oppose the Arms Trade or websites such as *The Tyee*, *Rabble*, *Upside Down World* or *The Dominion*.

The source for quotes and controversial facts is in the text along with the month and year. Because all the information in this book is easily accessible through a Google or Canadian Newsstand search, no endnotes have been included.

1. Tar Sands Diplomacy

No issue threatens humankind more than anthropogenic global warming. The American Meteorological Society says there is a 90 percent chance that global temperatures will rise by 3.5 to 7.4 degrees Celsius in less than one hundred years. The Climate Vulnerability Monitor claims climate disturbances are already responsible for as many as 350,000 deaths per year, a number expected to hit one million by 2030.

The World Meteorological Organization says there are clear links between climate change and the growing number of natural disasters. Climate change is exacerbating summer heat waves and wildfires. Rising temperatures may even be heightening volcanic and earthquake activity. Global warming is also predicted to devastate human health. The strong link between the distribution of pathogens and the environment means that climate change could lead to a massive increase in disease.

In many places global warming threatens food security. Over the past 250 years, oceans have absorbed more than 500 billion tons of CO_2. This has led to a 30 percent increase in the level of ocean acidity, which is threatening large and small crustaceans and endangering the food supply. If greenhouse gas emissions are not curbed, moderate drought is expected to affect half of the world by the end of the century. A Tyndall Centre for Climate Change Research study released at the end of 2010 found that global warming (rendering many areas uninhabitable) could lead to as many as a billion people losing their homes this century. Greenpeace, Oxfam and 18 other groups warned that global warming is a "phenomenon that threatens to reverse human

13

progress and make unachievable all UN targets to reduce global poverty." The world's poorest people are the primary victims of global warming. The great irony is that the countries most responsible for climate change are least affected. A March 2011 McGill University study confirmed that climate change would have the greatest impact on the countries that contribute the least to global warming. While Canada and the US, for instance, discharge among the most greenhouse gasses per capita, places like Bangladesh and Ethiopia will be hardest hit by climate change. During the December 2011 Durban conference on climate change campaigners dubbed growing carbon emissions a "death sentence for Africa". There is a growing climate justice movement focusing on the historic and ongoing injustices surrounding climate change.

Despite well-funded efforts to obfuscate the matter, a large body of scientific evidence suggests that human activity is responsible for rising temperatures. Long before he became Conservative environment minister, way back in January 1984, Peter Kent hosted, narrated and wrote a CBC television documentary called *The Greenhouse Effect and Planet Earth*. In the introduction, Kent said "the scientific community is virtually unanimous" that the planet is warming. He described "a change of climate that nature herself has not inflicted on the world since man has been in the world." Kent concluded: "The greenhouse effect must be considered as the world's greatest environmental concern." Since 1984 the evidence that human activity is driving global warming has become ever more persuasive. There is no longer any substantive dispute that climate change is occurring and that human activity is the cause. The question is not whether temperatures are increasing, but by how much and what effect this will have on our species survival. Will humanity increase the number of parts-per-

million of CO2 in the atmosphere until we imperil civilization? Or will we reverse course and hope the damage can be mitigated?

Despite the scientific evidence, and an overwhelming consensus among Canadians that something must be done to slow global warming, the Harper government has been at the forefront of efforts to block and reverse progress in this area. Canadian actions have spoken to the world. This country has become the lead cheerleader for Big Oil and their neoconservative agenda. Of course, in public Harper no longer disputes that human activity is responsible for climate change. This is a change from his previous position. For example, in a 2002 fundraising letter to Canadian Alliance supporters the new party leader wrote that the "Kyoto [Protocol] is essentially a socialist scheme to suck money out of wealth-producing nations." Harper claimed the accord was based on "tentative and contradictory scientific evidence" and called carbon dioxide "essential to life."

While he no longer publicly mocks the scientific consensus, Harper's actions as prime minister suggest he doesn't care if human activity is warming the planet. In fact, the Conservatives have stridently opposed attempts to regulate greenhouse gas emissions. At the end of 2011 Canada became the first country to withdraw from the Kyoto Protocol, an international agreement that committed the leading industrial economies to reducing their CO2 emissions below 1990 levels and to provide financial support for developing nations to follow suit. Governments and media outlets around the world criticized Canada's move. "France, China, Japan Hammer Canada Over Kyoto", noted a *CTV.ca* headline. A *Montréal Gazette* banner captured the international mood: "Kyoto rejection cements Canada's rogue reputation." Two months after the Conservatives' move the so-called BASIC countries (Brazil,

South Africa, India and China) wrote a joint letter criticizing Canada's withdrawal from Kyoto.

To justify the move the government claimed Canada would have to pay $14 billion in penalties to continue with the accord. In reality, Canada could have stayed in Kyoto without renewing the treaty, which is what Russia and Japan did. The Conservatives simply did not want to continue filing annual emissions reports, which showed that Canada was falling far short of meeting its emission-reduction targets. As this book went to print it was unclear if Harper planned to scrap all of this country's CO_2 monitoring programs. More generally, the Conservatives oppose all international efforts to curtail CO_2 if it means accepting binding commitments on Canada's greenhouse gas emissions.

The Conservatives' other justification for withdrawing was that China, India and other emerging fossil fuel consumers (as well as the US) were not restricted by the Kyoto Accord. Yet, weeks before the Conservatives announced their withdrawal China said it would make cuts to its emissions after 2020 and India agreed to an agreement with "legal force". "China's flexibility fails to alter Canada's Kyoto stance", was the *CTV.ca* headline. Ottawa's position was important as China said it was willing to cut its emissions only if rich countries extended their Kyoto commitments and helped poor countries implement low-carbon technologies. The Conservatives' move was one of the few times any country ever formally withdrew from an international treaty and, moreover, pulling out of Kyoto may have broken Canadian law. As this book went to press, the Conservatives' decision was being challenged in court.

Days before withdrawing from Kyoto, Canada led an effort to scuttle a follow-up agreement at a UN climate change

conference in South Africa. During the COP 17 (Conference of Parties) in Durban, Canada received six "fossil of the day" awards handed out by environmental groups to countries obstructing negotiations. It became so normal that on the day Canada did not receive the award Montreal daily *Le Devoir* ran a story about it. At the December 2011 conference Canada was also crowned with the "colossal fossil" for being "the country which has done the most day after day to prevent a climate treaty." This marked the fifth consecutive year Canada received this dubious honour given by 700 international civil society organizations from 90 countries. "I was astonished and disturbed by the comments of my colleague from Canada," said Indian environment minister Jayanthi Natarajan. She was especially upset that Peter Kent accused poorer countries of stalling the talks when Canada and other highly industrialized countries refused to sign the new, more rigorous, accord.

Before COP 17 the Conservatives made their hostility to a binding agreement on reducing CO_2 abundantly clear. In the lead up to the conference South Africa's High Commissioner in Ottawa, Mohau Pheko, complained to Postmedia that Kent was "bullying" and "arm-twisting" poorer countries in a bid to undermine the climate negotiations. In another interview Pheko said: "Are you going to follow the United States, are you also going to become a serial non-ratifier of any agreements?"

Responding to widespread criticism of Canada's position, Kent rejected what he termed "guilt payments" by rich countries for climate disturbances. In doing so the environment minister ignored the current and historical imbalances among countries' greenhouse gas emissions. According to a September 2009 *Guardian* comparison, Canada released 23,669 million metric tons of carbon dioxide between 1900 and 2004 while Afghanistan

released 77 million metric tons, Chad 7 million metric tons, Morocco 812 million metric tons and Egypt 3,079 million metric tons.

Even before withdrawing from Kyoto the Conservatives repeatedly sabotaged international climate negotiations. "Canada killing European effort to cut emissions" and "Canada blocking [Commonwealth] consensus on climate change," explained front-page *Globe and Mail* headlines concerning two different international meetings in 2007. In late 2008 *The Dominion* reported "the Climate Action Network named Canada the country most active in blocking, stalling or undermining the UN climate negotiations in Poland." At every turn Harper's government blocked progress on setting minimally serious targets for reducing CO_2 emissions or providing aid to poor countries to implement similar measures.

During the 2009 UN climate change conference in Copenhagen, Canada won eight "fossil of the day" awards and the "colossal fossil" award. Even more embarrassing, the Conservative government was targeted by the Yes Men, internationally renowned prankster activists. A week into the summit a press release from then environment minister Jim Prentice described Canada's "ambitious plan for a new climate change framework that answers vital concerns voiced by developing nations." It called for "strict new emissions-reductions guidelines for Canada" alongside generous "financing for vulnerable countries beginning in 2010." Simultaneously, the activists published a well-constructed facsimile of a *Wall Street Journal* article covering the Canadian press release. The fake article even included a business lobbyist criticizing Canada's purported announcement. Shortly after the surprise Canadian release a supposed 'Ugandan

delegation' convened a press conference. "This is the day that will define our century," said Margaret Matembe an MP and member of the Climate Committee of Uganda. "Today, we no longer have to wait for a COP20 or COP100 before the voices of our children are heard."

Soon after the supposed initial press release and the Ugandan press conference another press release denying the statement was issued: "OTTAWA, Ont. — December 14, 2009 — One hour ago, a spoof press release targeted Canada in order to generate hurtful rumours and mislead the Conference of Parties on Canada's positions on climate change, and to damage Canada's standing with the international business community. The Canadian government wishes to note that in addition to misleading the world on Canada's energy stance, today's impostors generated a cascading series of hopes that culminated in the delivery, by the Ugandan delegation, of an impassioned speech in today's COP 15 press briefing." This too was a fake. Designed to generate discussion or prompt a denial, it received significant media attention.

The Conservatives were not pleased. Harper's spokesperson Dimitri Soudas was filmed accusing (erroneously) well-known Québec environmentalist Steven Guilbeault of being responsible for the stunt. Later that day Steve Kelly, Prentice's chief of staff, was seen in a heated exchange with a US official over a seemingly innocuous opportunity for the press to photograph Canada's environment minister and lead US climate negotiator Steven Chu. The US official asked why the photo-op was so important; to which Kelly replied: "We were carpet bagged this morning by (environmentalists) with a false press release, I gotta change the story." In their effort to halt any further gimmicks the government pressed a web server to shut down the prankster's ISP

addresses, which crashed thousands of other websites. According to *The Greener Pages*, "the government strong armed an ISP into taking down the two fake sites — and simultaneously knock[ed] out 4,500 others in the process."

Opposed to international agreements to curtail greenhouse gas emissions, the Conservatives blocked domestic efforts as well. After the big stir created by environment minister Rona Ambrose's April 2006 declaration that Canada couldn't meet its Kyoto commitments, "Harper took a personal interest in the matter [reducing CO_2]," noted the *Globe and Mail*'s John Ibbitson in December 2011. "And that interest consisted of vetoing any meaningful action."

In November 2010 Harper got Conservative senators to kibosh the Climate Change Accountability Act passed by the three opposition parties while the Conservatives formed a minority government. The bill called for greenhouse gas emissions to be cut 25 percent below 1990 levels by 2020 and for bigger reductions over the longer term. Sent to the Senate for final approval the Climate Change Accountability Act was defeated without debate. For the first time in decades the Senate (known as the house of sober second thought) held a snap vote while 15 Liberal senators were away, defeating the bill 43 to 32. NDP leader Jack Layton called this move by unelected Conservative senators "one of the most undemocratic acts that we have ever seen in the Parliament of Canada."

As well as opposing attempts to reduce emissions the Conservatives undermined efforts to promote understanding of the issue. In 2007 they implemented new rules forcing Environment Canada scientists to get prior consent to speak to the media about their research. "Scientists have noticed a major reduction in the

number of requests, particularly from high profile media, who often have same-day deadlines," explained an internal Environment Canada document reported on by Canwest News in March 2010. "Media coverage of climate change science, our most high-profile issue, has been reduced by over 80 percent."

At the same time that they muzzled government scientists, the Conservatives cut funding for independent climate scientists. In early 2012 they eliminated the National Round Table on the Environment and the Economy, which produced reports that often challenged government policies on issues such as climate change. The Conservatives also chopped $117 million from the Canadian Foundation for Climate and Atmospheric Science (CFCAS), which supported 198 research projects that led to breakthroughs in climatology, among other fields. Contrary to government claims, money wasn't the issue. As they cut funding for climate research the Conservatives doled out huge sums for carbon capture research. This technology is designed to stop greenhouse gasses from escaping into the atmosphere during oil, gas and coal drilling. Alongside $2 billion from Alberta, in 2011 the Conservatives put up $650 million to help fund four carbon capture demonstration projects. Backed by the oil industry, these projects were largely designed to divert attention from the fundamentally unsustainable nature of the oil sands. In *Tar Sands: Dirty Oil and the Future of a Continent* Andrew Nikiforuk calls "[Carbon Capture and Storage (CCS)] a last ditch survival effort that defies economics and shirks logic. It extends the pretense that carbon is not connected to dirty oil and that business as usual in the tar sands is sustainable. It assumes that naive taxpayers will pick up the multibillion-dollar tab and that neighbouring communities will gladly assume the risks of living downwind from potentially leaky CCS cemeteries."

As a sign of the absurdity of the whole effort, in April 2012 the primary companies involved abandoned carbon capture efforts in Alberta. Despite immense amounts of government money, they said it still wouldn't be profitable.

Harper forcefully backs a corporate world and economic system driven by profits, conspicuous consumption and constant growth. These forces are hard to mesh with reducing greenhouse gas emissions. Moreover, the Conservatives are best friends with the companies profiting from the 'carbon bomb' better known as the tar sands.

Harper has deep ties to an Alberta oil industry profiting from this trillion dollar 'economic prize'. His father was an Imperial Oil executive and the future prime minister worked for the company as a young man. Calgary, with its downtown full of energy company offices, is where Harper went to university, began his political career and is the city he represents in the House of Commons. The prime minister tried to appoint close-friend Gwyn Morgan, the former CEO of EnCana, as the person in charge of government accountability (the opposition parties blocked it) while Harper's mentor at the University of Calgary, Barry Cooper, has been a Talisman Energy funded climate-change sceptic.

The Reform and Canadian Alliance parties, which morphed into Harper's Conservatives, traced their origins to the Trudeau government's National Energy Program (NEP) of 1980. In response to the NEP, outraged oil interests funded right-wing think tanks such as the Fraser Institute and built a Western-centric political alternative.

The Conservatives are also close to those leading the tar sands public relations battle. *Ethical Oil* author Ezra Levant gave up his party nomination in a Calgary riding for the Canadian Alliance

so the new head of the party, Stephen Harper, could run in a 2002 by-election. The individual who spun Levant's incredible defence of tar sands pollution into the ethicaloil.org campaign, Alykhan Velshi, worked for ministers Kenney and Baird. In 2012 Velshi became Harper's director of planning and made *Embassy's* list of the top 80 people influencing Canadian foreign policy. Conservative strategist Bruce Carson left the Prime Minister's Office (PMO) in 2008 to lobby for the tar sands. (Carson was charged with influence peddling in July 2012 for lobbying Aboriginal Affairs on behalf of his fiancée — a former escort 44 years his junior — who tried to sell water-purification systems to First Nations.) Described as a "grey-haired sage" and "probably the most strategic mind" in the PMO, in 2008 Carson became head of the Edmonton-based Canada School of Energy and the Environment. Started with $15 million in federal government money the year before, this think-tank was a collaboration among Alberta's three main universities. But, Carson's role was more "political" than "academic," according to Greenpeace Canada's Keith Stewart, who released a series of internal documents on the matter. Tied into both the political and business worlds, Carson was "the spider at the centre of the web" directing tar sands lobbying efforts. According to *The Tyee*, he "worked closely with Canada's biggest energy companies over past years to improve the public image of Alberta's oil sands." After a brief leave from the school in 2009 to return to the PMO, in March 2010 Carson (back at the School of Energy) met with the Canadian Association of Petroleum Producers and officials from the Alberta government and Natural Resources Canada to discuss a joint "outreach and communications" strategy for the tar sands. The public relations strategy discussed "would not just 'turn up the volume,'" according to briefing notes obtained

by Climate Action Network Canada, "it would change tact and address perceptions by showing that the issues are being addressed and we have the right attitude." In effect, they would respond to criticism of the tar sands but in a way that was more sophisticated than just dismissing environmental concerns. Carson co-authored a Canadian Association of Petroleum Producers briefing paper that argued "the economic and security value of oil sands expansion will likely outweigh the climate damage that oil sands create — but climate concerns are not to be ignored." The paper discussed US efforts to develop a Low Carbon Fuel Standard (LCFS), which "will need to be carefully monitored as [it] could have a potentially negative effect on oil sands imports." According to the paper, it was important for the industry to gain Ottawa's "support" to push back against any LCFS.

Conservative officials are defending one of the filthiest sources of fuel in the world. Tar sands oil extraction has been labeled one of the most environmentally destructive processes known to humankind. Viewed from above, the tar sands are as picturesque as a pair of dirty lungs and the stench of gasoline can be smelled for miles. Amidst a tangle of pipes, waste pools and smoke, an environmental demolition derby of 50-foot 300-tonne monster trucks roam a wasteland riddled with 200-feet deep open pits. Decked out with dinosaur-sized claws, Athabasca oil is mostly mined not pumped. In some areas the extraction process has scarred the earth beyond repair and the largely aboriginal communities living downstream have seen significant increases in cancer rates that have been attributed to the residues pumped into the Athabasca River. The resource intensive process of mining bitumen uses as much as two tonnes of sand to produce a single barrel of oil. Thousands of acres of trees have been clear-cut to

make way for tar sands mining and if current plans unfold, a forest the size of Maryland and Virginia will be eliminated. Cutting trees emits CO_2 and it also eliminates a carbon sink. A March 2012 Proceedings of the National Academy of Sciences study found that the destruction of Alberta's peat lands for tar sands production could release up to 173 million tonnes of CO_2, equal to as much as "seven years worth of mining and upgrading emissions at 2010 production levels."

A simple fact is that it takes two to three times more energy to extract a barrel of tar sands oil than a conventional barrel of crude. This is because a tremendous amount of energy is required to bring the oily sand to the surface and separate out a useful product. At 46 million tonnes of greenhouse gases a year — nearly as much as emitted by Norway — the tar sands represent far and away the biggest increase in Canadian carbon emissions. A July 2011 Environment Canada report showed that planned tar sands development would undo carbon-reductions from phasing out coal-based electricity and by 2020 tar sands emissions will constitute 12 percent of the country's total. "That's more than any province other than Alberta and Ontario, and is 40 percent more than Québec's total projected emissions in 2020," noted Simon Dyer, policy director at the Pembina Institute.

Already in 2007 greenhouse gas emissions from the oil sands were greater than the individual total from 145 of the 207 countries ranked. A Center for Global Development study found that fully developing the tar sands would devastate global food production, especially in climate vulnerable areas. Full exploitation of the tar sands would lead to a 5.6 percent loss in food productivity with countries such as Ethiopia, Sudan and heavily populated India worst affected. The Center for Global Development report

explains: "There is striking asymmetry in regional impacts. Full exploitation of the oil sands deposit by Canada, a high-income country, would have the most severe impacts on regions where the poorest countries are concentrated."

Many apologists claim the industry has cleaned up its act since the explosion of tar sands production in the mid-2000s. But privately, according to an internal memo unearthed by Postmedia, Environment Canada admits it has no "credible scientific information on [the tar sands industry's] environmental performance", and this "was affecting the industry's ability to raise capital from and sell into (the) foreign market." Rather than reducing the sector's footprint, future production will be more energy intensive as the most accessible bitumen was extracted first. An Environment Canada memo released in February 2012 explained: "While the industry has taken steps to reduce emissions, the shift from mining to in situ production, which is almost three times as emissions intensive as mining, is resulting in a continued acceleration of emissions from this sector." Future production will be concentrated in northern Alberta's Carbonate Triangle, a 27,000 square mile area lying deep below the surface that contains about a quarter of the province's bitumen.

The rapid growth of the tar sands has unleashed an important international political battle. On one side sits the Conservative government, a plethora of right-wing think tanks and some of the richest companies in the world. On the other side are a mass of individuals, First Nations and environmental organizations appalled by the tar sands' mammoth ecological toll.

During a short trip to London in November 2011 this author received an unexpected taste of the ongoing battle. At a student demonstration against rising tuition fees someone handed

me a leaflet announcing a public discussion focused on how "the UK government has recently bowed to Canadian government and industry pressure and are trying to undermine The European Fuel Quality Directive, which would effectively ban tar sands from being sold in Europe." A few minutes after receiving the leaflet I read a Kings College newspaper story about students disrupting a speech by Joe Oliver, Canada's natural resources minister. A group called People and Planet took the stage before Oliver's lecture at the London School of Economics to present the minister with an award for "Greenwash Propagandist of the Year."

Expanding oil production from the tar sands has spurred significant grassroots activism in the British capital and around the world. When Alberta energy minister Ron Liepert visited London in January 2011, protesters gathered outside the Canadian High Commission. In May 2012 dozens of cities in thirteen countries participated in the third annual "Stop the Tar Sands" day of action. At the end of 2011 several prominent South Africans, including anti-apartheid hero Archbishop Desmond Tutu, criticized Alberta's dirty oil in a full-page *Globe and Mail* advertisement. "For us in Africa, climate change is a life and death issue. By dramatically increasing Canada's global warming pollution, tar sands mining and drilling makes the problem worse, and exposes millions of Africans to more devastating drought and famine today and in the years to come." In Norway the tar sands became an election issue because many people disagreed with state-owned energy company Statoil's Alberta investments. "It's been an issue for political debates and also for the media," Gunnar Kvassheim of Norway's Liberal party, told Canadian Press during the September 2009 election. "It's been one of the environmental issues that have been focused on in this campaign." When he visited Norway in the fall

of 2009 environment minister Jim Prentice was struck by public hostility towards Statoil's investment in the tar sands. He later told US ambassador David Jacobsen, according to a diplomatic cable released by Wikileaks, that the experience "heightened his awareness of the negative consequences to Canada's historically 'green' standing on the world stage." Prentice told the US ambassador in Ottawa the Conservatives were "too slow" in responding to the dirty oil label and "failed to grasp the magnitude of the situation." A confidential August 2010 email from London-based Canadian diplomat Sushma Gera echoed this sentiment. "The oil sands are posing a growing reputational problem, with the oil sands defining the Canadian brand," Gera wrote. "With [a] recent increase in the NGO campaigns targeting [the European] public, we anticipate increased risk to Canadian interests much beyond the oil sands."

The Conservatives responded to this growing international indignation with intensive lobbying efforts. The Conservative government, argued independent journalist Martin Lukas, "has become the foreign branch of the tar sands industry."

A few months after Prentice's trip to Europe, Foreign Affairs laid out a Pan-European Oil Sands Advocacy Strategy to "protect and advance Canadian interests related to the oil sands" through a "reframing of the European debate on oil sands". According to internal documents, Canadian embassies tailored messages for each country "based on lines from Ottawa", which would focus on government efforts to reduce the industry's environmental and social toll. As part of the strategy Canadian diplomats monitored environmental activism, offered trips to Alberta, sponsored conferences, paid for public relations services to combat "significant negative media coverage" and shared

"intelligence" with "likeminded allies" BP, Statoil, Total and Shell, which have "huge investments" in Alberta. In August 2010 the Pan-European Oil Sands team reported: "Oslo [Canadian embassy in Norway] holds regular meetings with Statoil to update on each others' activities and coordinate where appropriate. Hague is enhancing its engagement with the private sector and met with Shell recently. Paris has regular meetings with Total ... London is also in regular contact with the private sector including meetings with Shell, BP and Royal Bank of Scotland as well as Canadian oil companies." In June 2010 Harper met Total's chief executive Christophe de Margerie when he visited Paris. One can only assume this was part of the Conservatives "engagement with the private sector" mentioned above.

The government also trained Canadian diplomats to promote the tar sands. A February 2011 retreat brought diplomats from 13 different European offices together with a number of federal government departments, Alberta's energy minister and representatives from Total, Shell, Statoil and the Canadian Association of Petroleum Producers. At this "training" diplomats were given "an industry perspective" as well as information on the federal and Alberta government positions. An email summarizing this meeting to officials from Foreign Affairs, Environment Canada and Natural Resources Canada explained: "Two key messages from day one were: oil sands advocacy in Europe is now recognized as a priority for all concerned; and there is a clear need for regular in-house training to equip those of us on the ground with the expertise to deal with this highly technical file."

One goal of the Pan-European Oil Sands Advocacy Strategy, according to a March 2011 document obtained by Climate Action Network Canada, was to "target" European politicians –

"especially from the ruling and influential parties" – to oppose a European Union plan to implement a Fuel Quality Directive. The Fuel Quality Directive would force suppliers to shun tar sands oil in favour of lower-emission fuels. Since Europe does not import tar sands oil the legislation would have little direct effect on the industry but it could set a precedent to be copied elsewhere. "While Europe is not an important market for oil sands-derived products, Europe legislation/regulation, such as the EU Fuel Quality Directive, has the potential to impact the industry globally," a Canadian diplomat in London, Kumar Gupta, explained in an April 2011 email released through access to information legislation.

This country's diplomats lobbied forcefully against the EU Fuel Quality Directive's designation for the tar sands. Friends of the Earth Europe found that Canadian officials met British and European representatives 110 times between September 2009 and July 2011 in a bid to derail the new fuel legislation. The goal was to ensure "non-discriminatory market access for oil sands-derived products", according to documents uncovered by Friends of the Earth. Chris Davies, a British member of the European parliament, told Reuters in May 2012 that Canada's lobbying campaign "has been stunning in its intensity." Highlighting the unique nature of Canada's campaign, Satu Hassi, a Finnish MP, said: "There have been massive lobbying campaigns by the car industry, by the chemicals industry, banks, food giants, etc. But so far I have not seen such a lobbying campaign by any state."

In their bid to exempt the tar sands from the Fuel Quality Directive the Conservatives openly threatened European officials. "[Resources minister] Oliver warns EU climate policies could disrupt oil supply" noted a March 2012 Postmedia headline, while a February 2012 *Ottawa Citizen* title explained "Canada threatens

trade war with EU ahead of oilsands vote." In an early 2012 letter to the EU, David Plunkett, Canada's ambassador to the EU, wrote: "If the final measures single out oil sands crude in a discriminatory, arbitrary or unscientific way, or are otherwise inconsistent with the EU's international trade obligations, I want to state that Canada will explore every avenue at its disposal to defend its interests, including at the World Trade Organisation."

The Conservatives' strategy bore fruit. The EU delayed its original deadline of January 2011 for confirming baseline default values on different fuels. "A vote in Brussels", noted the *Globe and Mail* in February 2012, "gave the Canadian government a win in its battle to preserve international markets for oil sands producers against an environmental lobbying effort, which wants refiners worldwide to pay financial penalties for using the carbon-intensive Alberta crude as well as other sources of 'dirty' fuel." After the vote Friends of the Earth Europe spokesperson Darek Urbaniak complained: "some European governments have given in to Canadian and oil lobby pressure, instead of saying no to climate-hostile tar sands."

As part of their tar sands focus Canada's diplomatic apparatus in Europe became hyper sensitive about environmental issues. In the summer of 2011 internationally recognized Toronto artist Franke James accused the Conservatives of undermining her planned European tour because she publicly criticized the tar sands. "Feds Tried to Sabotage Climate Change Art Show: Artist", noted a *Tyee* headline. A major corporate sponsor cancelled $75,000 in funding, James learned, because "a Canadian official called and persuaded them to withdraw from sponsoring the exhibition." Around the same time a trade commissioner at the Berlin embassy, who was previously enthusiastic about the exhibition, suddenly

became "evasive and contradictory". Without corporate and government money the planned tour was cancelled. The Croatian non-profit that planned a travelling art show of James' meditations on "green conscience" — alongside talks on climate change — was furious. A statement from Nektarina Non Profit said they felt "patronized" and "intimidated" by the "interventions of the Canadian government."

While the issue is sensitive in Europe it is opposition to the tar sands down south that most concerns the Conservatives. An internal March 2009 Natural Resources Canada power-point presentation worried that "US legislation at both federal and state levels potentially target oil sands production" while a November 2010 Foreign Affairs memo described how the "[oil sands] industry is under ferocious attack by the US environmental movement." The Conservatives worked feverishly to beat back US legislation that might curtail tar sands expansion, establishing the United States Oil Sands Advocacy Strategy. According to *Embassy*, "some suggest that the energy file is by far the biggest issue that the Canadian-US diplomatic network deals with, and consumes the most personnel and resources." A Foreign Affairs spokesperson refused *Embassy*'s August 2010 request to break down the resources devoted to tar sands lobbying. "What I can tell you is that numerous employees in the Canadian Embassy's Washington Advocacy Secretariat, which includes the Province of Alberta's office, are engaged in various aspects of energy advocacy, as is the Ambassador and other sections within the Embassy." Both *Maisonneuve* magazine and *The Tyee* published articles detailing Ambassador Gary Doer's voluminous efforts on behalf of the tar sands. "Doer has devoted much of his professional energy to promoting the oil sands industry, flying to industry roundtables, meeting with US policymakers,

and speaking to national magazines," noted *Tyee* reporter Geoff Dembicki in an April 2011 article that was part of a series dubbed the "The War for the Oil Sands in Washington."

Conservative lobbying targeted both federal and state policies to reduce carbon emissions from fuel. In 2007 California governor Arnold Schwarzenegger signed the world's first Low Carbon Fuel Standard (LCFS) into law. The bill mandated California's Air Resources Board (CARB) to assign carbon footprints to different fuels in a bid to deter oil suppliers from using high-carbon fuel sources. CARB's standard was set to take effect in January 2011. According to Dembicki, Canadian officials intervened at least five times to affect how California defined its LCFS. In February 2008, then Canadian ambassador Michael Wilson wrote CARB chairman Mary D. Nichols asking her not to unfairly target the tar sands. Government emails obtained by Climate Action Network Canada suggest Wilson's letter was part of a tar sands "advocacy strategy" developed by three federal departments in late 2008. As part of this strategy natural resources minister Lisa Raitt wrote governor Schwarzenegger in April 2009. "While your LCFS regulation will be for the State of California alone, we realize that it could serve as a model for other states and perhaps the United States federal government. ... The [Canadian] Government recommends that the LCFS regulation should assign all mainstream crude oil fuel pathways the same CI [carbon intensity] rather than distinguish among different sources of crude oil."

A group that worked closely with the Canadian embassy in their pro tar sands fight, the Center for North American Energy Security, and two other groups sued California to repeal the LCFS. In part, they argued that the policy would "harm our nation's energy security by discouraging the use of Canadian crude oil."

The first phase of the lawsuit was successful and at the end of 2011 California was forced to postpone its LCFS until a higher court could adjudicate the matter.

When this book went to press no other state had passed a LCFS. When Wisconsin proposed a LCFS in its Clean Energy Jobs Act of 2010 Canadian officials formally intervened. Canadian consuls Brian Herman and Georges Rioux read a statement before the State's Senate Select Committee on Clean Energy. "I would like to leave you with one request," Rioux told the Wisconsin legislators. "While you pursue new energy policies including a potential [LCFS] please ask the question: Will this result in Wisconsin becoming more dependent on oil from Saudi Arabia, Iraq and Venezuela because we've cut off supply from our northern neighbours, our friends and allies?" Heavily dependent on Canadian oil, Wisconsin abandoned its LCFS three months after Herman and Rioux intervened.

In a bid to keep LCFSs off the political agenda Canadian diplomats lobbied state governors. By March 2009 Alberta's envoy at the embassy in Washington, Gary Mar, had visited more than 20 state governors, noted *The Tyee*. After the Republicans triumphed in the 2010 mid-term elections Canadian officials hosted "an informal breakfast to honour Governors and Governors-Elect" at the W Hotel near the White House. At the November 15 event Ambassador Doer communicated the federal government's perspective on energy issues.

The Conservatives' concern with any individual state passing a LCFS went beyond any direct impact on tar sands production. They feared that if a growing number of states implemented this type of legislation the US Congress could eventually regulate the carbon emissions of transportation fuel. This

would undermine tar sands development. The Conservatives first target in the US was an obscure piece of federal legislation signed into law by President George W. Bush at the end of 2007. Section 526 of the Energy Security and Independence Act effectively forbids government agencies, including the heavy consuming US military, from buying oil with a high carbon footprint. According to internal emails unearthed by the Pembina Institute, a few weeks after Section 526 was passed, Canadian embassy officials alerted the American Petroleum Institute, Exxon Mobil, BP, Chevron, Marathon, Devon and Encana. "As yours is a company involved in the production of oil sands in Canada," then-energy counsellor Paul Connors wrote an Exxon Mobil lobbyist, "I wanted to bring this issue [526] to your attention."

To monitor the provision the American Petroleum Institute formed a committee, which immediately met representatives from the Canadian embassy and Alberta's Washington office. Embassy officials worked with the American Petroleum Institute and the Center for North American Energy Security, a creation of the American Petroleum Institute, to ensure that 526 would not apply to the tar sands as was intended by Democratic Congressman Henry Waxman who introduced that section of the Energy Security and Independence Act.

In addition to building a coalition of domestic oil lobbyists, Canadian officials protested Section 526 through official diplomatic channels in Ottawa. Ambassador Michael Wilson communicated Canada's objection to having 526 apply to the oil sands to the Secretary of Defense (the US Department of Defense is far and away the largest government purchaser of fossil fuels). Canadian and Alberta officials also met top US military officials and Congress members about 526.

Canadian officials feared that 526 could set an "important precedent" for wider bans on tar sands oil, according to internal emails the Pembina Institute obtained. "We hope that we can find a solution to ensure that the oil keeps a-flowing," wrote an official at the embassy in Washington in February 2008. Canadian energy counsellor Paul Connors described the longer term fear to an Exxon lobbyist: "We see the debate on Section 526 as part of a larger debate by some to have the US consider either a tailpipe or a lifecycle low carbon fuel standard (Lieberman-Warner) for transportation fuels." For its part, Alberta hired a Washington lobbyist in 2009 to "provide advice for dealing with initiatives that could affect our interests (e.g. the next Section 526)."

While Section 526 of the Energy Security and Independence Act was a small step towards improving government purchasing habits Barak Obama campaigned on a pledge to enact a LCFS. The Conservatives were none too pleased. Three months before the fall 2008 election Conservative cabinet minister Tony Clement and executives from Calgary-based Nexen Energy met Obama's top energy advisor Jason Grumet during the Democratic National Convention in Denver. Though details of the meeting were not released, the public statements by Clement and Nexen vice president Dwain Lingenfelter give an indication of the meeting's tone. Clement said: "We [the Conservative government] have to be more aggressive in representing Canadian values and interests in the American political scene." For his part, Lingenfelter told the press after the meeting with Obama's top energy advisor: "If you don't like the oil sands oil, what companies will do [in Canada] is build a bigger pipeline to the west coast and export it to China and India." Early drafts of President Obama's 2009 climate bill contained provisions for measuring the emissions created by

36

producing different types of fuel. Internal documents show that Canadian policymakers worried this might negatively impact the country's interests. As such, they worked with oil interests to stop it.

A December 2011 *Salon.com* article titled "Big Oil and Canada thwarted US carbon standards" detailed Canadian and oil industry lobbying to water down the legislation, particularly the LCFS. The article explained: "Canadian embassy officials worked closely with the planet's wealthiest oil companies to weaken the section's language, and in some cases, to repeal the bill entirely... helping to blunt President Obama's climate change agenda. And few outside of the Canadian embassy were any wiser."

The Conservatives' bid to weaken US climate legislation were particularly disingenuous since they argued against reducing CO_2 emissions on the grounds that any Canadian move without concurrent action from our largest trading partner would lead to economic ruin. Ruling out any unilateral action on climate change, environment minister Jim Prentice told a November 2008 business forum: "We will seek to work closely with the new US administration to build the North American low-carbon economy." He reiterated the point in October 2009. "The North American economy is integrated to the point where it makes absolutely no sense to proceed without harmonizing and aligning a range of principles, policies, regulations and standards. We will only adopt a cap-and-trade regime if the US signals that it will do the same. Canada's position on harmonization applies equally to regulation."

The Harper government lobbied most vigorously in support of Calgary-based TransCanada's plan to build a $7 billion pipeline to take oil from Alberta to refineries on the Gulf Coast of the US. The US environmental movement mounted significant

opposition, pressing Obama to deny the company a permit to construct the Keystone XL pipeline. Protesters dogged the president on the issue throughout 2011 and in August of that year 1,250 people were arrested during two weeks of anti-pipeline civil disobedience in Washington D.C. In November 2011 some 15,000 pipeline opponents surrounded the White House.

Appalled that the pipeline might be rejected, Harper fought back ferociously. On a number of occasions the prime minister pressed Obama to approve Keystone XL while a number of ministers visited Washington to press the matter with Secretary of State Hillary Clinton. Immigration minister Jason Kenney tweeted in September 2011: "Keystone pipeline will offset US imports of Venezuelan oil w/CDN oil. Why does the left prefer Hugo Chavez oil to CDN's ethical oil?"

Ambassador Doer spent a large amount of his time pushing the pipeline. He responded to critical press commentary and pressed state officials to support Keystone XL. When Nebraska's Republican governor Dave Heineman came out against the pipeline Doer visited him in Omaha. Similarly, the 28 members of congress who urged the State Department to consider the "major environmental and health hazards" posed by Keystone XL received an immediate letter from Canada's ambassador and Alberta's minister of intergovernmental relations. "I believe it necessary to address several points in your letter which require clarification," Ambassador Doer wrote. The ambassador's letter trumpeted Canada's plan to reduce overall greenhouse gas emissions 17 percent below 2005 levels by 2020. "[This is] a benchmark we intend to meet," Doer wrote, knowing full well that planned tar sands expansion would make this objective impossible to reach.

The Tyee described the intensity of Canadian lobbying efforts on behalf of Keystone XL. One congressional aide compared Canadian officials to "aggressive" car salesmen. It "was the most direct encounter I've had with a lobbyist representing a foreign nation," a congressional staffer told the online news site. In January 2012 *Globe and Mail* columnist Jeffrey Simpson wrote: "The Harper government put Canada's entire diplomatic apparatus in the US behind the Keystone campaign." Canada's 22 consular offices in the US were ordered to take up the cause. When the *New York Times* ran an editorial titled "say no to the Keystone XL" Canada's consul general in New York wrote a letter supporting the project.

Those who thought consular officials spend their days helping hard-pressed individuals retrieve lost documents or extricate themselves from difficult circumstances may be surprised that it turns out Canada's diplomats are really on the frontline of advocacy for dirty oil.

2. Mining the World

"Canadians are justly proud of our mining industry for its elevated sense of corporate social responsibility."

Stephen Harper, April 2012, Cartagena, Colombia

"Canada's mining sector leads the world in responsible mining practices."

Foreign Affairs spokesperson Me'shel Gulliver Bélanger
May 2012, Ottawa

Who cares that Canadian diplomacy is used to promote the interests of big oil companies, a cynic might say. We need to look after our own self-interest and exploiting the oil sands provides good jobs to many Canadians. This may be true if you only consider a narrow economic perspective and are prepared to ignore global warming. But how do Canadians feel about diplomacy that facilitates razing mountaintops, poisoning rivers and ignoring indigenous rights in dozens of countries around the world? Do most of us want our tax dollars promoting the narrow self-interest of wealthy shareholders at the expense of common people living in some poor part of the world? Unfortunately, with overseas mining the golden rule of 'do unto others as you would have them do unto you' has been trumped by the reality of 'out of sight, out of mind'.

Canada is a global mining powerhouse. Nearly 60 percent of the world's mining companies are listed on this country's stock exchanges and as much as 80 percent of global mining equity financing takes place in Canada. The industry has grown rapidly over the past decade. Canadian mining companies' overseas investments increased from $30 billion in 2002 to $210 billion

in 2011, according to the *Canadian Mining Journal*. Most of this growth was in Latin America, Asia and Africa where corporations operate under limited oversight.

As a result there have been an astounding number of conflicts at Canadian-run mines. Throughout 2009/10 the Standing Committee on Foreign Affairs and International Development heard accounts about dozens of different mining conflicts. On November 23, 2009, former Argentine environment minister Romina Picolotti told the committee her staff was "physically threatened" after pursuing environmental concerns about a project run by the world's largest gold producer, Toronto-based Barrick. "My children were threatened. My offices were wiretapped. My staff was bought and the public officials that once controlled Barrick for me became paid employees of Barrick Gold."

At least Picolotti wasn't murdered. A month after her testimony, on December 21 and 26, two activists opposed to a Vancouver-based Pacific Rim Mining project in El Salvador were killed (three others were also killed). Violence wasn't the only means employed. The company established a US subsidiary so it could sue El Salvador through the US-Central America free trade agreement for refusing to approve the mine's permits.

Less than a month before the back-to-back killings in El Salvador three current and former employees of Calgary-based Blackfire Exploration allegedly murdered Mariano Abarca Roblero, who led opposition to the company's mine in Chicomuselo, a small municipality in the Mexican state of Chiapas. In response 250 demonstrated in front of the Canadian embassy in Mexico City and 2,500 marched in Chicomuselo. On a pre-planned visit to Chiapas, Governor-General Michaëlle Jean and deputy foreign minister Peter Kent were greeted with chants of "Canada get out."

This hostility may shock Canadians lulled into ignorance by this country's dominant political culture, but it should not surprise government officials. Mexico's second biggest paper *La Jornada* regularly covered the destruction caused by Canadian mines and in July 2009 Canadian Press unearthed an internal government memorandum explaining: "Given the sheer number of Canadian mining companies operating in Mexico . . . it is highly likely that the embassy will be increasingly implicated in disputes between mine activists and Canadian mining companies operating in Mexico."

No matter how much Canadians wish we were simply known for hockey or our comedians, the mining industry increasingly represents Canada abroad. Canadian mining corporations operate thousands of projects outside this country and many of these mines have displaced communities, destroyed ecosystems and provoked violence. Pick almost any country in the Global South — from Papua New Guinea to Ghana, Ecuador and the Philippines — and you will find a Canadian-run mine that has caused environmental devastation or been the scene of violent confrontations. There have been so many conflicts that even the industry associations effectively admit the problem. A leaked report commissioned by the Toronto-based Prospectors and Developers Association of Canada found that Canadian companies were responsible for a third of 171 high-profile Corporate Social Responsibility (CSR) violations surveyed by mining companies between 1999 and 2009. The report concluded: "Canadian companies have been the most significant group involved in unfortunate incidents in the developing world. Canadian companies have played a much more major role than their peers from Australia, the United Kingdom and the United

States. Canadian companies are more likely to be engaged in community conflict, environmental and unethical behaviour."

This doesn't seem to bother the Harper government, which is close to the most retrograde sectors of the industry. In early 2007 a pan-Canadian roundtable launched by the previous Liberal government crossed the country to interview a wide variety of social actors about Canadian mining. The roundtable put forward 27 recommendations to better address the human rights and environmental effects of Canadian companies operating abroad. Mining Watch explained: "The final CSR package at the core of the 2007 Advisory Group report included comprehensive human rights norms in the standards set, and the possibility of sanction (but not remedy) in the form of withholding of government financial and political support for companies found by the Ombudsman and Compliance Review Committee not to be living up to the adopted standards."

Even though the Mining Association of Canada helped formulate the 27 recommendations — and tepidly agreed to them — other powerful forces opposed the plan. Barrick Gold, which operates some of the most controversial mines in the world, the Prospectors and Developers Association of Canada and the Canadian Chamber of Commerce lobbied the Conservatives to reject the roundtable's recommendations. They found a sympathetic ear. After stalling on the issue for two years, in March 2009 trade minister Stockwell Day rejected the roundtable's proposal to make diplomatic and financial support for resource companies operating overseas contingent upon socially responsible conduct.

When it became clear the Conservatives would not act on the 2007 roundtable's recommendations, Liberal MP John McKay introduced An Act Respecting Corporate Accountability for the

Activities of Mining, Oil or Gas Corporations in Developing Countries (Bill C300). The bill was designed to codify into law a number of the main recommendations from the 2007 roundtable. Under Bill C300 companies that failed to adhere to (relatively lenient) standards of social responsibility would lose the support of Canadian embassy officials and taxpayer-funded agencies such as Export Development Canada, a crown corporation that provides billions of dollars of insurance and advice to companies operating outside of the country.

This private members bill made it to its third, and final, reading before the House of Commons. Once the mining industry realized Bill C300 had a realistic chance of becoming law — controversial private members bills rarely pass — they launched a ferocious lobbying campaign. According to *CBC.ca*, this included nearly 300 visits by registered lobbyists representing Barrick Gold, Vale Canada, IAMGOLD and the Prospectors and Developers Association of Canada. Harper whipped his MPs into opposing the bill, which enabled industry lobbyists to blitz 15 Liberal MPs with a request to abstain on a bill submitted by a member of their party. On October 27, 2010, the House voted 140 to 134 against Bill C300. The voting ran along on party lines with almost every Conservative MP voting against it and the opposition parties voting in favour. But 13 Liberal MPs, four from the NDP and six Bloc members failed to show up for the vote (one independent opposed the bill and another abstained).

In the following election campaign the Liberal, NDP and Green platforms all included plans to strengthen rules to ensure that Canadian mining companies live up to international human rights and environmental standards. The Conservatives' platform did not. Their position was that voluntary standards, despite

45

countless horror stories suggesting the contrary, were the best way to improve mining companies' social responsibility. When minister Day publicly rejected the roundtable's 27 recommendations he said there was no need for additional measures to control Canadian resource companies operating abroad. "Most Canadian companies have set standards for social responsibility when they go into another country," Day told reporters. "We want to see best practices highlighted and set out there as the benchmarks that companies should reach for." This was a pointed reversal of the Conservatives domestic law and order agenda. That party always seems to argue that the best way to curtail anti-social behaviour by individuals is to impose stiffer sentences (negative reinforcement), yet here Day argued that the socially destructive practices of corporations could be overcome by highlighting these authoritarian institutions' good works (positive reinforcement).

As part of their promotion of voluntary efforts the government launched Building the Canadian Advantage: A Corporate Social Responsibility Strategy for the Canadian International Extractive Sector. In October 2009 they established an Extractive Sector Corporate Social Responsibility Counsellor with a $620,000 budget to probe complaints about abuses committed by Canadian companies in poor countries. But, the Counsellor could not intervene — let alone take any remedial action — without agreement from the company accused of abuse. By late 2011 the Toronto-based CSR Counsellor's office had received only two complaints, noted *CBC.ca*, "one of which was dropped because the mining corporation chose not to undergo the voluntary investigation."

The person Stockwell Day appointed as the initial CSR Counsellor, Marketa Evans, was the founding director of the

University of Toronto's Munk Centre for International Studies. Established with funding from Peter Munk, chairman and founder of Barrick Gold, the billionaire maintained significant influence over the Centre with its director reporting to a board set up by the Munk family. Munk espoused far-right political views. He defended Chilean dictator Augusto Pinochet and virulently attacked Venezuelan president Hugo Chavez. In a March 2011 *Globe and Mail* interview he dismissed criticism of Barrick's security force in Papua New Guinea, which led Norway's pension fund to divest from the company, by claiming "gang rape is a cultural habit" in that country.

As time passed, the Conservatives' CSR strategy increasingly rested on diverting government funds to promoting mining interests. In 2012, reported the *Ottawa Citizen*, Foreign Affairs spent hundreds of thousands of dollars to bring journalists from Latin America and Mongolia to the Prospectors and Developers Association of Canada conference and to tour mines in Québec. The Harper government created the Investment Cooperation (INC), a $20 million program "designed to support responsible business investment in developing countries and thus reduce poverty and promote economic growth." INC was mainly supposed to help companies investigate the likely social consequences of an investment. According to the government, "program applicants and clients must demonstrate adherence to strict international corporate social responsibility (CSR) standards in order to receive funding." The standards clearly weren't "strict" as INC contributed $270,000 in September 2010 to the controversial operations of Centerra Gold in Mongolia. Centerra was criticized for its mining operations across the border in Kyrgyzstan where a worker was crushed to death and a number

of large chemical spills caused 2,500 illnesses and a handful of deaths. In March 2012 a number of Mongolian and international organizations (Mining Watch, the United Mongolian Movement of Rivers and Lakes, Rights and Accountability in Development etc.) complained to Canada's National Contact Point for the OECD Guidelines about Centerra's failure to respect Mongolian laws. (At one point that government suspended the company's license.)

Between 2006 and early 2012 CIDA approved at least $50-million in projects linked to the mining industry, according to a *Globe and Mail* investigation of the organization's project database. International development minister Bev Oda aggressively defended CIDA's support for mining companies in interviews and at the 2012 Prospectors and Developers Association of Canada conference in Toronto, which was attended by five Conservative ministers. Oda told the mining bigwigs they were "making significant investments in development projects and improving the quality of life for thousands in countries where you work. ... The mining industry is a huge contributor to a nation's wealth and is one of the main building blocks of civilization." She ended her speech by saying: "I look forward to learning from your industry on how to improve the effectiveness of Canada's development work internationally, and to working more closely together to create a better life for those living in poverty."

Through Canada's Corporate Social Responsibility Strategy for the Canadian International Extractive Sector the government put up $27 million in 2011 for projects in Colombia, Peru, Bolivia, Ghana and Burkina Faso. CIDA said its partnership with mining companies was designed to "improv[e] the competitive advantage of Canadian international extractive sector companies by enhancing their ability to manage social and environmental

risks." One example of the aid agency's efforts was a $4.5-million grant to Lundin for Africa, the philanthropic arm of mining giant Lundin Group of Companies. Another example was the $20 million Andean Regional Initiative in Peru, Bolivia and Colombia intended to "promote corporate social responsibility through partnership arrangements between extractive sector companies and other stakeholders aimed at socioeconomic development and support to governance."

As part of their Corporate Social Responsibility Strategy for the Canadian International Extractive Sector the government also strengthened the bonds between mining companies and non-governmental organizations (NGOs). In June 2011 CIDA announced $6.7 million in funding for collaborative efforts between three leading mining companies and NGOs. The biggest of the projects was between Plan Canada and IAMGOLD. "In Burkina Faso," according to the government release, "CIDA is supporting Plan Canada, and its partner IAMGOLD, in implementing a job skills training project in 13 communities to meet labour market demands in a variety of sectors, including the mining sector and its sub-sectors." The government put $5.7 million into the project while IAMGOLD invested $1 million and Plan Canada spent $900,000.

The goal of the CIDA-funded project, the head of training programs at Burkina Faso's education ministry told the *Globe and Mail* in March 2012, was to "respond to the needs of the mining company." Adama Traore added that "a number of graduates are expected to go directly into jobs at the mining company."

The Plan Canada-IAMGOLD training took place in a charged political context. To scare its workers, in May 2011 IAMGOLD closed its Essakane mine in Burkina Faso. The

company's CEO, Steve Letwin, warned the miners: "I have zero tolerance for strikes that are illegal. And, as they [the workers] will find out, will not tolerate anything that has a negative impact on our stakeholders." In March 2012 Bloomberg reported that 100 people protesting a lack of local employment at the Essakane mine were scattered by the police.

These protests help explain why the company sees the CIDA-funded job training as helpful. The same day Bloomberg reported protests at the mine site Letwin was quoted in the *Globe and Mail* saying that youth unemployment in the community was a major obstacle for the company as "over the course of time, they're [youth] going to want more of a take", which could mean "increased taxes and royalties" for IAMGOLD.

The two other NGO-mining company projects announced by CIDA in mid-2011 were substantially smaller. The aid agency allocated $500,000 to a project between World University Service of Canada and Rio Tinto ALCAN "to provide direct skills training to 400 young people to help diversify the local economy within mining communities." Together the company and NGO put up another $428,000 for the project. CIDA also invested $500,000 in a World Vision Canada/Barrick Gold project. "In Peru," noted the aid agency, "CIDA is supporting World Vision Canada, in a program that will increase the income and standard of living of 1,000 families affected by mining operations." World Vision and Barrick combined to match CIDA's donation. In response Miguel Palacin, the head of a Peruvian indigenous organization, sent a letter to World Vision, Barrick and CIDA claiming that "no 'social works' carried out with the mining companies can compensate for the damage done, particularly in the face of rights having been violated."

Writing in *Embassy* Rick Arnold, former coordinator for Common Frontiers-Canada, summarized Palacin's criticism: "For this World Vision-led 'development' project to go ahead in the district of Quiruvilca in the face of concerted opposition locally and nationally would be tantamount to running a pacification program, and not a development project, in advance of the eventual destruction of a people's way of life—all for gold."

CIDA-funded NGO-mining contracts are problematic for a number of reasons. First, taxpayers should not subsidize the social responsibilities of highly profitable mining companies. In addition to this obvious point, such CIDA contracts further weaken NGOs critical of Canadian operations while strengthening those groups willing to defend and work with mining companies. After a debate erupted over CIDA's funding of NGO-mining projects, the three above mentioned NGOs defended their ties to industry in the *Globe and Mail*. Signed by the heads of World University Service of Canada, Plan Canada and World Vision Canada the opening sentence of the January 2012 op-ed read: "Canadian [mining] companies are major drivers of economic growth in the global South." It went on to note, "These companies are already significant development actors in their own right."

Another downside of this sort of CIDA funding is that it places the moral weight of the aid agency (and NGOs) on the side of the company. Mark Mattner, a PhD Candidate at McGill University, wrote: "operating in partnership with CIDA implies an ethical stamp of approval for particular projects. What could be wrong with an extractive project if the government finances development projects that are associated with it?" This is obviously the case with a specific mine but is also true at a broader political level. Tying Canadian aid funding to mining projects strengthens

the political forces in the recipient countries supportive of the extractive industry all the while weakening critical voices.

Time and again Harper has used diplomatic trips to support controversial mining projects. Barrick gained important support for its Pascua Lama operations, which spurred large-scale protests, during his July 2007 trip to Chile. The prime minister visited the company's Chilean office and said: "Barrick follows Canadian standards of corporate social responsibility." He was greeted with signs from mine opponents stating "Harper go home" and "Canada: What's HARPERing here?"

During a November 2007 visit to Tanzania Harper once again met representatives of Barrick, which had more than $1 billion invested in the East African country. Days before meeting the prime minister, Barrick officials claimed a strike at one of its Tanzanian mines was illegal and looked to replace a thousand striking miners. To protect its North Mara mine Barrick employed 300 security officers — and paid part of the salary for two dozen police officers — linked to seven violent deaths from July 2005 to late 2008. The October 2011 *Globe and Mail Business* magazine reported on a Tanzanian lawyer organization's claim that 19 villagers were killed by police and security guards at the North Mara mine between January 2009 and June 2010. The victims were usually searching for gold.

Under Harper all levels of Canadian diplomacy have promoted mining. Anthony Bebbington, director of the Graduate School of Geography at Clark University, told the Standing Committee on Foreign Affairs and International Development in February 2012 that a "sub-secretary in a [Latin American] ministry of energy and mines" told him "as far as I can tell, the Canadian ambassador here is a representative for Canadian mining

companies." The Massachusetts-based academic also quoted an unnamed Latin American environment minister, who complained about Canadian lobbying and mining, saying: "I don't know if Canada has been quite so discredited in its history." Bebbington's report to the Standing Committee fits a larger pattern. In Ecuador Canadian officials took a keen interest in the country's mining debate after large-scale mining was suspended for 180 days while a new mining law was written in 2009. The senior vice-president of EcuaCorriente, one of the Canadian companies bitterly opposed by local communities, described the diplomatic effort. Ian Harris wrote: "The Canadian Embassy in Ecuador has worked tirelessly to affect change in the mining policy — including facilitating high-level meetings between Canadian mining companies and President Rafael Correa."

Along with a number of mining representatives, Canada's ambassador to Ecuador, Christian LaPointe, discussed mining regulations with Ecuador's president in April 2008. According to *CBC.ca*, LaPointe "attended the meeting with the mining companies and presented the Canadian government's concerns over the mining rules." To add to the embassy's efforts trade minister Stockwell Day traveled to Ecuador in August 2009. During the visit Day said: "It was important for me to be here to promote our leadership in this [mining] sector. Whether it is protecting the environment, helping communities or respecting the position of Indigenous peoples, we think responsibility and economic prosperity can go hand in hand."

The Conservatives' lobbying was successful. Canadian businessmen were granted a privileged position during mining law negotiations and key Canadian holdings escaped Ecuador's mining mandate.

Further south, the Conservatives signed a free trade agreement largely to protect $5 billion in Canadian mining investment in Peru from the type of legislative changes Ecuador implemented. Signed in the midst of intense mining conflict, the 2010 trade agreement — with environmental and labour safeguards "even weaker than NAFTA's" — was designed to remove any future Peruvian government's ability to change mining regulations or to expropriate the properties of Canadian companies. In June 2011 indigenous Aymara in eastern Peru led a wave of anti-mining protests. Six protesters were killed when 1,000 demonstrators tried to occupy the Inca Manco Capac Airport near Lake Titicaca. In response to the protests the Ministry of Mines and Energy withdrew Vancouver-based Bear Creek Mining's concession to develop a silver deposit. After the company's concession was withdrawn Bear Creek CEO Andrew Swarthout threatened the Ministry. "There's a free-trade agreement between Canada and Peru which is very regulated, so there's avenues there," Swarthout told Agence France Presse. "We will go through the free trade agreement."

The Conservatives have demonstrated particular interest in Peru's mining sector. In 2008 CIDA gave $4 million to the Mineral Resources Reform Project to provide technical assistance and technological support to Peru's Ministry of Mines and Energy. The official goal of the Mineral Resources Reform Project was "development of activities oriented to the consolidation of the institutional capacity of the sector, which means the services provided by the Ministry of Mines and Energy, and to contribute to the generation of greater confidence in the Ministry and its regional offices." CIDA's push to improve the prospects for Canadian mining corporations through the Mineral Resources Reform Project warranted a visit in early 2008 by the minister of

international cooperation. *Embassy* reported: "Ms. [Bev Oda] … arrived in Peru meeting with the Latin American nation's energy and mines minister, as well as Canadian and Peruvian mining companies and NGOs to discuss mining sector reform." Partly to facilitate Canadian mining investment, in 2009 CIDA chose Peru as one of its 20 "countries of focus" and after meeting new president Ollanta Humala in November 2011 Harper announced a four-year $4.9 million Conflict Management and Prevention in the Extractive Sector (COMPES) project to "help promote economic growth in Peru by reducing the impact of social conflicts related to the use of natural resources."

On the other side of the world from Peru, Afghanistan's natural resources may have influenced Canadian military policy in that country. "Is mineral-rich Afghanistan the next mining hotspot?" asked a March 2008 *Financial Post* headline. The Conservatives brought the Afghan minister of mines to the Prospectors and Developers Association of Canada Conference in Toronto. "Minister Adel," a Foreign Affairs invitation to the conference promised, "will speak about the tremendous mining opportunities in Afghanistan, including details on a number of projects. He welcomes the opportunity to meet with Canadian companies."

In November 2011 the Afghan Ministry of Mines awarded Toronto-based Kilo Goldmines a 25 percent stake in Hajigak, the largest iron deposit in Asia. The Conservatives hailed the move. "Canada is strongly committed to helping Afghans rebuild their country, and this investment by Kilo Goldmines will create jobs and prosperity for Afghans and Canadians alike," said trade minister Fast. "As the first significant engagement of a Western firm in the Afghan mining sector, this project will enable hard-

working Canadians from Canada's world-class mining sector to help Afghanistan develop its mining infrastructure, which will lead to further growth and opportunities in both the Afghan and Canadian economies."

In at least one case the Conservatives established diplomatic relations with a country simply to serve mining interests. In April 2008 Agence France Presse reported: "Canada will establish a new trade mission in Ulaanbaatar, Mongolia, this year to help Canadian companies active in the region's mining sector." Three months after that the trade mission was expanded to full embassy status. Canadian diplomatic representation in Mongolia was necessary because, according to Ted Menzies, parliamentary secretary to the minister of finance, "there have been some policy issues including taxation, control and investment regulations that have put Canadian companies in the region in an extremely challenging position." Soon after the Conservatives established the embassy they began to negotiate a foreign investment promotion and protection agreement to "provide greater predictability and certainty for Canadian investors considering investment opportunities in Mongolia."

With some 20 Canadian mining companies active in the country, Canada was the second largest investor in Mongolia. Ottawa's biggest concern was Vancouver-based Ivanhoe, which owned a copper and gold project in the Gobi desert. This $6 billion project, noted the *Financial Post*, "was the major campaign issue" in Mongolia's 2008 election. In April 2006 at least 3,000 people marched against foreign mining in Mongolia's capital, with protesters burning an effigy of Ivanhoe's Robert Friedland. The ire directed towards Friedland was partly because of comments he made in 2005. Friedland explained his Mongolian venture to an

investor's conference this way: "So we're coming in from outer space and landing at Oyu Tolgoi ... And the nice thing about this: there's no people around; the land is flat, there's no tropical jungle; there's no NGOs. We're only 70 kilometres from the Chinese border. It does not snow here. You've got lots of room for waste dumps." The company also took heat for loaning $50 million to the government in exchange for tax concessions.

The Conservatives actively lobbied the Mongolian government on behalf of Ivanhoe. A *Globe and Mail* Report on Business headline described a January 2008 trip to Mongolia by trade minister David Emerson (who joined the board of a mining company after he left public office): "Emerson to push for Ivanhoe deal in Mongolia." As part of its efforts to woo the country's decision-makers, the Conservatives doled out tens of millions of dollars in aid to Mongolia. In August 2011 development minister Oda visited Mongolia and CIDA ramped up its funding to a country with limited historic ties to Canada.

In middle of 2012 opposition to Vancouver-based South American Silver's operations in central Bolivia grew. Weeks of protest against the junior mining company culminated with a handful of people being sequestered and an indigenous activist's death on July 6. This prompted the Bolivian government to nationalize South American Silver's mine. The Conservatives immediately went to bat for the company. After the death, trade minister Ed Fast sent a letter to the Bolivian government expressing "deep concern" over reports it might nationalize the company's operations. Fast's spokesman Rudy Husny told the *Vancouver Sun* the trade minister instructed Canadian officials to "intensify their engagement with the Bolivian government in order to protect and defend Canadian interests and seek a productive resolution

of this matter." This included visits with officials in La Paz and Bolivia's ambassador to Canada. An August 2012 statement from South American Silver noted: "The Company thanks the Canadian government for its strong support by raising this matter as a priority on a number of diplomatic fronts."

The most egregious case of the Conservatives defending mining interests took place in the Democratic Republic of the Congo (DRC), a country that's had its natural resources viciously exploited by foreigners for over a century. Claiming Vancouver-based First Quantum violated parts of its contract, in September 2009 the Congolese government withdrew the company's rights to a copper mine in the eastern part of the country. The Conservatives staunchly defended First Quantum. "Canada to press Congo mining dispute at G20 meeting", noted London's *Financial Times* several months later. At the G8/G20 in June 2010, the Conservatives pushed for a declaration to the final communiqué calling on the Congo to "extend urgently the rule of law" and "enhance governance and accountability in the extractive sector." The *Financial Post* captured the mood: "G8 leaders scold Congo on governance." A First Quantum spokesperson told the paper: "The company is encouraged by the G8's statement regarding the governance issues challenging the resource sector in the [DRC]." But the Conservatives did not stop there. They also took the issue to other international forums. The *Financial Post* reported: "Harper will raise the case of Vancouver-based First Quantum Minerals Ltd. with representatives from the World Bank, the International Monetary Fund and other governments that do business in the DRC." As part of this effort, Ottawa obstructed international efforts to reschedule the country's foreign debt, which was mostly accrued during more than three decades of Joseph Mobuto's

dictatorship and the subsequent multi-country war. "The Canadian government wants to use the Paris Club [of debtor nations] in order to resolve a particular problem [with First Quantum]", explained Congolese information minister Lambert Mende in November 2009. "This is unacceptable." Ottawa refused to respond directly to allegations that it used Congo's indebtedness to gain political concessions for Canadian mining companies. But, Conservative government spokesperson Me'shel Gulliver Bélanger told Reuters: "Some Canadian firms have been having significant issues in a challenging investment environment."

A *Canadian Business* article based on a number of access to information requests noted that First Quantum hired Daniel Brock, a lawyer who formerly worked in the Finance and Foreign Affairs departments. "Brock met twice with officials, including the international trade minister's chief of staff, to discuss 'Canadian foreign policy regarding debt forgiveness package for Democratic Republic of Congo.'"

After winning concessions that pleased Canada's many mining companies in the Congo, Ottawa relented on the debt rescheduling. While it was largely ignored outside of this country's business press, the story received significant attention "in the Congo where newspaper editorial cartoons mocked Canada and First Quantum", reported the *Financial Post*.

Aside from *Canadian Business* and *The Dominion* the Canadian media seem to have ignored the circumstances under which First Quantum acquired its concession. Apparently, the company made a deal with a rebel leader, Laurent Kabila, fighting the national government in the mid-1990s. One reason First Quantum's project was nationalized is that the company rejected the Congolese government's attempt to renegotiate mining licenses

granted during the 1998-2003 multi-country war. An October 2002 report by the UN Panel of Experts on the Illegal Exploitation of Natural Resources and Other Forms of Wealth of the Democratic Republic of the Congo accused First Quantum of violating OECD guidelines during the war. The report referred to the "collusion" between foreign mining companies and "highly placed government officials who provide mining licences and export permits in return for private gain. ... For example, in its attempts to buy rights to the Kolwezi Tailings, First Quantum Minerals (FQM) of Canada offered a down payment to the State of $100 million, cash payments and shares held in trust for Government officials. According to documents in the possession of the Panel, the payments list included the National Security Minister, Mwenze Kongolo; the Director of the National Intelligence Agency, Didier Kazadi Nyembwe; the Director General of Gécamines, Yumba Monga; and the former Minister of the Presidency, Pierre-Victor Mpoyo. The FQM share offer to those officials was premised on a sharp rise in its share price once it was announced that it had secured some of the most valuable mineral concessions in the Democratic Republic of the Congo."

So, it would appear that not only do the Conservatives support the interests of the mining industry in general, but under Harper this country's foreign policy enforces the interests of all mining companies, no matter the context. Is this a foreign policy to make Canadians proud?

3. Against the Arab Spring

The divergence of Harper's foreign policy from the principles and norms of ordinary Canadians is apparent not only in the Conservatives' uncritical support of oil and mining companies, but also in other aspects of what most of us would consider traditional diplomacy — government to government relations. Nowhere is this divergence more clear than in North Africa and the Middle East, the focus of the next few chapters. Here the reasons for Harper's foreign policy may be more complex than the straightforward promotion of wealthy people's financial interests.

On December 17, 2010, a Tunisian street vendor set himself ablaze to protest harassment by municipal officials in the town of Sidi Bouzid. Mohamed Bouazizi's death sparked a month-long protest movement that toppled the 23-year dictatorship of Zine El Abidine Ben Ali. But Harper stuck with the Tunisian president to the bitter end. The Conservatives never called on Ben Ali to resign and largely ignored the regime's repression, which saw over 200 people killed and thousands more hurt or arrested during the uprising. On January 7 the front page of *Le Devoir* asked: «M. Harper, où êtes-vous?». The paper reported on a protest the day before where a hundred members of Montréal's Tunisian community demonstrated against Ben Ali and in favour of international pressure to restrain the regime. A member of the Tunisian Solidarity Collective told the Montréal daily: "Harper where are you? How many will have to die before you say anything about the situation in Tunisia?"

According to internal documents acquired by Postmedia, on December 30 Freedom House asked Foreign Affairs to make

a statement on the "ever-worsening situation" in Tunisia. The Conservatives stalled, waiting for the US/European reaction to Ben Ali's repression. "Given that like-minded (allies) have not issued statements and the time lag since events, we do not see a strong rationale to issue something now," one internal email explained. "Please keep us posted should you hear of further developments [among allies]."

Twenty-six days after the protests began, on January 12, Foreign Affairs finally released a somewhat tepid statement. "Canada is concerned by the deterioration of peaceful demonstrations in Tunisia into widespread violence. We are particularly concerned by reports of violence during public rallies, where many people have died, others have been wounded and a large number have been arrested. Canada urges the Tunisian authorities to restrain their security forces and to engage in an open dialogue with civil society to seek solutions to the social and economic problems the country is facing. Canada believes that respect for human rights and democracy are necessary to ensure peace, prosperity and security in Tunisia."

Two days later, after Ben Ali stepped down on January 14, the government issued a second press release. "Canada regrets the loss of life in the last month of violence in Tunisia and extends its sincere sympathies to the families of the victims. Canada welcomes news that free elections will be held in the near future, which will give all Tunisians a voice in building a new government committed to democracy, human rights and the rule of law."

When this statement was released long-time Prime Minister Mohamed Ghannouchi was still in place and members of Ben Ali's Constitutional Democratic Rally (RCD) party controlled key ministries. Did the Conservatives hope the basic nature of the

Tunisian regime could be preserved, but with a new figurehead? If so, their position was thwarted by further demonstrations and the resignation of all non-RCD ministers, which forced the expulsion of the remaining RCD ministers two weeks later.

After backing Ben Ali until the end the Conservatives tried to claim they supported democracy in Tunisia. "Canada supports the transition in Tunisia," Harper told the press during a trip to Morocco on January 26. "We support the democratic development that is taking place there and obviously want to see that proceed positively." Once Ben Ali fled and his regime collapsed, Harper loudly opposed attempts by the dictator's family to take up refuge in Montréal. "Ben Ali's family not welcome in Canada: Harper", noted a headline about Ben Ali's billionaire brother-in-law Belhassen Trabelsi's Canadian property and citizenship. In a sign of the government's successful obfuscation a Google search of Harper's ties to Ben Ali elicits a great deal of information about the Conservatives moves to stop the dictator's family from staying in Canada and almost nothing about their support for Ben Ali until his final hours in office. Similarly, the Conservatives announced they were freezing Trabelsi's assets in Canada, but once the media lost interest in the issue the Conservatives appear to have dropped it. A year and a half after Ben Ali fell the Conservatives had not returned millions of dollars in frozen assets to the Tunisian treasury.

Harper's after-the-fact outrage cannot hide the government's support for Ben Ali. Fifteen months before the protests began (22 years into Ben Ali's rule) foreign minister Cannon visited Prime Minister Ghannouchi and Foreign Minister Abdelwaheb Abdallah in Tunis. "My meetings with the Prime Minister and Foreign Minister were very productive, reflecting our close ties," noted Cannon. At the time of Ben Ali's fall the two

countries were negotiating a foreign investment promotion and protection agreement and two months before the protests began Export Development Canada released a glowing assessment of Tunisia's investment climate. Detailed in *Le Devoir* ten days after the dictator fled, EDC's report "reassured" potential Canadian investors by claiming the "regime of President Ben Ali is staying the course and maintaining Tunisia's political stability, thanks to its special attention to social welfare and, in parallel, the force and effectiveness of the national security forces." The EDC report added that fortunately "most of the Islamist opposition has left the country or been imprisoned."

Tunisia was not the only country where Canada was on the wrong side of the movement towards democracy. The demonstrations quickly spread to neighbouring Arab states. "The people want to bring down the regime" was a call shared by many. On January 25 Egyptians began 18 days of protest, including widespread labour actions, which would topple the 30-year presidency of Hosni Mubarak. Canadians from coast to coast were gripped by scenes of protesters standing down security forces in Cairo's Tahrir Square. Many were also excited at the prospect of 80 million Egyptians throwing off the yoke of dictatorship. Not the Conservatives though, who were largely concerned about Israel, not the embattled Egyptian population.

For the first three days of this internationally televised conflict the Conservatives ignored the protests and state repression. On January 27, Cannon said "Canada regrets the loss of life of both protestors and police officers during political demonstrations in Egypt. We urge all parties to refrain from violence, and, in particular, we urge the Egyptian authorities to respond to these protests peacefully. … Egypt remains an important partner for

Canada, and we urge the Egyptian government to ensure full freedom of political expression for its citizens."

Four weeks earlier the Conservatives took a much stronger position when 21 Coptic Christians (seen as Mubarak supporters) were killed in a church bombing. After that incident in Alexandria, Cannon said in a statement: "We fully support the call by Egypt's President Hosni Mubarak to close ranks and confront the terrorists who were behind this deplorable attack."

Six days into the Egyptian protests, on February 1, Mubarak announced that he would not contest an election due in September. He also promised constitutional reform. Most protesters were not satisfied and anti-regime demonstrations continued the next day. In response, stick-wielding Mubarak loyalists on camels and horses charged into Tahrir Square in a bid to dislodge the protesters. Several civilians were killed and 1,500 hurt in "The Battle of the Camels". Even after these well-publicized clashes Harper backed Mubarak's transition plan. On February 3 the *Globe and Mail* reported "[Harper] endorsed the go-slow transition plan set out by Egyptian President Hosni Mubarak's regime, signalling that Mideast stability and peace with Israel are its paramount concerns while other Western nations push for faster change."

The Conservatives stuck with Mubarak until literally the last possible minute. On February 10 Foreign Affairs called for "restraint from all parties to settle the crisis" and about three hours before Mubarak's resignation was announced on February 11 Harper told a Newfoundland audience: "Our strong recommendations to those in power would be to lead change. To be part of it and to make a bright future happen for the people of Egypt." The PM failed to call for Mubarak's immediate departure.

Most of Canada's traditional allies abandoned Mubarak before the Conservatives. The day after he stepped down Alec Castonguay explained in *Le Devoir*: "Canada was the only Western country to not call for an 'immediate transition' in Egypt. While Washington, London, Paris, Madrid and Rome openly called for an end to Mubarak's rule and the transfer of power to a provisional government, Ottawa sided with Israel in refusing to condemn the old dictator."

To a certain extent the Conservatives followed US statements. One academic told the *Globe and Mail* that Ottawa's position was a "lagging indicator of US policy." But, Israel was the Conservative's main focus. After Mubarak fell senior *Globe and Mail* columnist Jeffrey Simpson explained: "The Harper government, once again seeing the Middle East through the exclusive prism of Israel's interest, remained throughout so hesitant, cautious and, frankly, on the wrong side of history in commenting on Egyptian developments. Better the dictatorship we know than the democracy we don't seemed to be the Israeli and Canadian position." A week into the protests, on February 2, the Canada-Israel Committee sent a document to deputies and ministers calling on them to support "stability" in Egypt based on "a future that's not simply more democratic but where that democracy is guided by such values as non-violence, the rule of law, and respect for human rights, including the rights of religious minorities." Effectively, the Canada-Israel Committee was saying that 80 million Egyptians should live under dictatorship so the 'only democracy in the Middle East' can more securely occupy Palestinian and Syrian territory.

The Conservatives lauded Egypt's peace treaty with Israel. During an August 2009 visit to Cairo, minister Cannon

noted Canada's "support for its [Egypt's] key role in helping to bring about long-term peace in the Middle East." Hours after Mubarak stepped down Harper said: "We will also continue to encourage and support Egypt's efforts to promote regional stability and peace, including with Israel as well as continued respect for peace treaties in the Middle East."

The US-sponsored Egypt-Israel peace treaty was designed to remove Egypt from the Arab-Israeli conflict. Much reviled by ordinary Egyptians, the 1979 treaty effectively allowed Israel to attack Palestinians, Syrians and Lebanese without fear that the largest Arab country would intervene.

Mubarak's fall spurred protesters throughout the region. Tens of thousands took to the streets against pro-US monarchies in Jordan, Bahrain, Morocco, Saudi Arabia and elsewhere. Largely to appease international opinion, the leadership in these countries announced cosmetic reforms. At the same time they clamped down on protests. Thousands were arrested and dozens killed by security forces. Notwithstanding a few mild criticisms, the Conservatives applauded the monarchies' cosmetic reforms. In an end of 2011 interview with *Diplomat and International Canada* foreign minister Baird explained: "[Morocco] King Mohammed VI really embraced reform in a big way. King Abdullah II in Jordan has really expedited reforms they were already working on. In Saudi Arabia, you've got to support every step forward. The decision to grant women the right to vote in local elections was a positive step. I'd like to see them go much farther."

Baird's positive portrayal of the reforms doesn't withstand scrutiny. All three countries remained monarchies with power concentrated in the hands of a ruling clique. In Saudi Arabia labour unions are outlawed while in Morocco and Jordan they are heavily

restricted. Much the same can be said for independent media and in all three countries elections mean little. While Baird lauded the Saudi king for granting women the right to vote in municipal elections, scheduled for 2015, he ignored the fact that municipal officials have almost no power.

During a November 2011 visit to Kuwait and the United Arab Emirates (UAE) where Baird "took part in discussions about important developments in the Middle East and North Africa region", the foreign minister praised these US-backed monarchies. "Canada will continue to support people who are seeking to bring freedom, democracy, human rights and the rule of law to their respective countries." Baird stressed that "Canada will continue to protect Canada's interests and promote Canadians' values around the world. Religious freedoms and the role of women in civil society are two incredibly important features to safeguard in these new and emerging democracies." In response, *Jewishindependent. ca* noted: "Baird's comments are a bit confusing. Neither UAE or Kuwait are true democracies, nor do their leaders appear to be seeking the things Baird says we support, including women's rights in the way that most Canadians would find acceptable. Neither is a beacon of religious freedoms. If anything, Baird's comments sound like he is putting commercial interests ahead of the human values he himself raises as important."

Two weeks after Ben Ali fell in Tunisia Harper visited Morocco on a planned trip to Switzerland. During his visit Harper "launched formal free trade negotiations with Morocco" and had "an audience with Moroccan King Mohammed VI." The prime minister acknowledged discussing the regional protests with Morocco's leadership, telling a *Toronto Star* reporter he valued the regime's perspective on "developments in this part of the world."

Days before the prime minister arrived, on January 26, four Moroccans protesting the cost of food set themselves alight and in subsequent weeks tens of thousands would take to the streets demanding social and political reforms. Not one of Foreign Affairs' 200 press releases in 2011 spoke in favour of Morocco's democracy movement or criticized the government for arresting hundreds of protesters. In February 2012 a Moroccan activist found guilty of "insulting the king" was given three years in jail and a large fine. There was no word from Ottawa about this repression, the imprisonment of many student leaders or the fact that Morocco banned TV station *Al-Jazeera*.

The Conservatives were also silent about Jordanian democracy struggles. In March and April 2011 thousands of Jordanians marched against the monarchy and for better social conditions. A handful of protesters were killed and hundreds arrested in a country that prosecutes individuals for "extending one's tongue" (having a big mouth) against the King. Ottawa failed to criticize its long-standing ally with whom the Conservatives had concluded a free-trade accord, which the government noted "shows Canada's support for Jordan as a moderate Arab state that promotes peace and security in the Middle East." In addition to the trade accord, the Jordanian military benefited from Canadian weaponry. Among other deliveries, Canadian companies sent $105,000 in small arms ammunition in 2009 and a $5.3 million radio encryption management system financed through the Canadian Commercial Corporation.

Some of the largest "Arab Spring" demonstrations took place in a small island nation sandwiched between Saudi Arabia and Qatar. Three days after Mubarak stepped down in Egypt major protests broke out against the 217-year-old monarchy in

Bahrain. Protesters initially focused on greater political freedom and equality for the majority Shia Muslim population, but after security forces killed four and injured dozens on February 17, calls for the king to go grew more common. To its credit Foreign Affairs released a mildly critical statement the day after this widely publicized crackdown. "Canada regrets the loss of life in Bahrain and calls on all parties to refrain from violence. We urge the Bahraini authorities to exercise restraint, and we encourage the Bahraini government to promptly investigate the deaths of protesters. Canada urges Bahrain to respect its citizens' rights to freedom of expression and assembly, and to engage in peaceful dialogue with its people to address their concerns."

Over the next month, protests against the monarchy gained in strength with 200,000, a quarter of the country's adult population, marching on February 22, 2011. The regime looked to foreign security forces for protection. They brought in Sunni Muslims from Pakistan and after a month of growing protests 1,500 troops from Saudi Arabia and the UAE were sent to shore up the Al Khalifa regime. A day after these well-armed foreign soldiers arrived, the Bahraini king declared martial law and a three-month state of emergency. That same day, March 15, Bahraini security forces killed two more demonstrators and within days protesters camped out in central Manama's Pearl Roundabout were violently dispersed, leaving five dead and hundreds wounded. The regime also began late night raids in Shia neighbourhoods. They arrested thousands, including bloggers, internationally recognized human rights activists and doctors accused of caring for injured protesters.

Three days after the foreign intervention Ottawa (ever so) subtly criticized the Saudi invasion as well as the regime's repression and martial law. "Canada is concerned by the recent

evolution of the situation in Bahrain and urges all parties to renounce any recourse to violence. We also call on Bahrain and the countries of the Gulf Cooperation Council to exercise the utmost restraint and maintain an environment favourable to democratic reform. Canada urges the Government of Bahrain to protect the safety of demonstrators and return to fully respecting their freedom of assembly. We strongly encourage Bahraini authorities to continue their efforts toward building a sincere dialogue that addresses the concerns of the country's citizens." This Canadian statement failed to explicitly condemn the Saudi invasion, call for democratic reform in Bahrain or back the protesters demand that the king go. Foreign Affairs did not release any further press release on the political situation in Bahrain even though the regime continued to brutally repress protesters throughout 2011 and early 2012. According to a February 2012 *Ottawa Citizen* report, some 90 protesters were killed or disappeared in the year following the protests and "twenty-seven Shia shrines and mosques were destroyed as part of the government's response. In secret trials, protesters were sentenced to death, mainstream politicians arrested, nurses and doctors who treated injured demonstrators were jailed and the country's only opposition paper closed."

On March 20, 2011, Ottawa resident Naser Al Raas was detained by officers from Bahrain's interior ministry as he was boarding a flight out of the country. For weeks government officials denied knowledge of the former Microsoft IT specialist. Al Raas was then released, but without his passport. Initially accused of kidnapping a police officer, Al Raas was sentenced to five years in prison for breaking the country's illegal assembly laws. For 10 months the Harper government remained silent on the matter. Three months into the ordeal Al Raas' fiancée told *Global Research*: "We are begging

the Canadian government to please do something ... please help us. For God's sake, this innocent Canadian citizen is being tortured by a barbaric regime and Mr. Harper has not even bothered to lift the phone." For his part, Al Raas said: "I feel abandoned by my government. I have done nothing wrong yet I have been tortured and now face prison. I am terrified that I will be tortured again."

It was not until he was sentenced to five years in prison in February 2012 that deputy foreign minister Diane Ablonczy criticized Bahrain's treatment of Al Raas and when the charges were dropped she immediately congratulated the regime. "We would like to express our appreciation to the Bahraini authorities for, in the case of Mr. Al-Raas, applying the recommendations made by the Bahrain Independent Commission of Inquiry to ensure, among other things, free political expression and protection from arbitrary detention."

Why the Canadian deference to such a small country? Home to the US Fifth Fleet, Bahrain is an important Western ally. In October 2008 Canadian naval vessel commander Bob Davidson handed command of Operation Enduring Freedom's Combined Task Force 150 to the Danish Navy in Manama, Bahrain. Dignitaries from that country as well as Saudi Arabia, Yemen, Britain, Denmark and the US attended the event. "The ceremony," noted Patrick Lennox in *FrontLine Defence Magazine*, "highlighted Canada's strength and good will to a region in which we are a relative newcomer. These are the kind of events that help Canada open new doors for our commercial interests and for the promotion of our values." The Conservatives strengthened business relations with Bahrain. In February 2010 they concluded a foreign investment promotion and protection agreement with that country. According to Foreign Affairs, Bahrain "offers significant investment

opportunities for Canadian investors in a variety of sectors, including education, infrastructure and healthcare."

But the real key to explaining the Canadian government's actions is Saudi Arabia, which has the world's largest known oil reserves. "A stupendous source of strategic power, and one of the greatest material prizes in world history" is how the US State Department described Saudi resources in 1945. Since then Saudi Arabia has been tied into the US geopolitical orbit even if it is one of the most misogynistic and repressive countries in the world with the Qur'an ostensibly acting as the constitution. Outside its borders, the Saudi royal family uses its immense wealth to promote and fund many of the most reactionary, anti-women social forces in the world. They aggressively opposed the "Arab Spring", spending huge sums to undermine democratic change. The Saudi-led Gulf Cooperation Council (GCC) — a political and economic alliance that includes the monarchies of Kuwait, the UAE, Oman, Bahrain and Qatar — launched a counterrevolution that included military support for the monarchy in Bahrain, disinformation through their ownership of Arab media and financial support for reactionary groups in Tunisia and Egypt. At the same time the GCC backed the foreign military intervention in Libya and armed the opposition to Bashar Assad in a bid to remove Syria from the Iran/Hezbollah/Shia orbit. The Saudi monarchy may be the worst regime in the world. (The US, of course, is responsible for far more violence but it is relatively free domestically. North Korea is as repressive but its foreign policy is benign compared to Saudi Arabia's.) The Conservatives' ties to the Saudi monarchy demonstrate the absurdity (even on their terms) of Harper's claim that "we are taking strong, principled positions in our dealings with other nations, whether popular or not."

The Conservatives have been extremely deferential towards the Saudis. When defence minister and deputy premier Crown Prince Sultan bin Abdulaziz Al Saud died in October 2011 foreign minister Baird gushed with praise. "On behalf of all Canadians, I extend my deepest condolences to the Custodian of the Two Holy Mosques, King Abdullah bin Abdulaziz Al Saud, to the Royal Family and to the people of Saudi Arabia. The Kingdom has lost a man of great achievement who dedicated his life to the well-being of its people."

Appointed defence and aviation minister in 1962, Prince Sultan bin Abdulaziz Al Saud was a leading figure in the country for five decades. He oversaw the kingdom's support for North Yemen's monarchists during that country's bloody civil war in the 1960s and he pushed a stridently anti-communist position. Bin Abdulaziz Al Saud rebuked US President Jimmy Carter for his "pusillanimity" (cowardliness) in response to the 1979 Soviet invasion of Afghanistan. Implicated in a number of major corruption scandals, bin Abdulaziz Al Saud made Saudi Arabia the largest importer of US arms, strengthening the country's role as a Western military ally. His son, who was the Saudi ambassador in Washington for 22 years, developed notoriously close ties with US presidents George H.W. Bush and George W. Bush.

When Crown Prince Nayef bin Abdul-Aziz Al Saud died in June 2012 Baird once again issued a glowing assessment. "Saudi Arabia has lost an honourable man of great achievement who has dedicated his life to the security and prosperity of the people of Saudi Arabia." In fact, Nayef bin Abdul-Aziz Al Saud, interior minister for three and a half decades, was considered a fairly conservative member of the Al Saud family. He resisted the weakening of Wahhabi religious doctrine as a threat to the

monarchy's grip on power. His motto was "no to change, yes to development" and in March 2009 he publicly opposed both elections and women in government.

The Conservatives released two press releases praising the lives of Saudi princes but they stayed quiet when the regime took the lives of "Arab Spring" protesters. This author could find no direct Canadian criticism of Saudi Arabia's role in crushing the democracy movement in Bahrain. In April 2011 the UK *Observer* reported: "Evidence has emerged that Saudi forces have been involved in violence against the opposition in the mainly Shia villages and suburbs around Manama. In a graphic eyewitness account of the repression given to the *Observer*, a Bahraini who has been caught up in the violence claimed that officers with Saudi accents, in plainclothes but armed with automatic weapons, had led attacks on members of the Shia opposition on several occasions over the past month."

Nor did the Conservatives release any statement about the Saudi's domestic repression. Alongside the upsurge in protest across the region, small numbers demonstrated in Riyadh and other major centres. They were quickly disbursed in what Amnesty International called a new "wave of repression" that saw hundreds of reformists arrested and imprisoned after "grossly unfair" trials. "Peaceful protesters and supporters of political reform in the country have been targeted for arrest in an attempt to stamp out the kinds of call for reform that have echoed across the region," said Amnesty's Middle East director Philip Luther in December 2011. Human Rights Watch reported: "Saudi Arabia responded with unflinching repression to demands by citizens for greater democracy in the wake of the pro-democracy Arab Spring movements."

Security forces allegedly killed Faisal Ahmed Abdul-Ahad, a leading organizer of a Facebook group that attracted 26,000 members and planned a 'Day of Rage' protest against the regime in Riyadh on March 2. At least six men languished in jail for their involvement in the planned demonstration, Amnesty reported in a briefing paper titled *Saudi Arabia's 'Day of Rage': One year on*. On March 5, 2011, the Saudi monarchy reasserted its ban on all demonstrations. "Regulations in the kingdom forbid categorically all sorts of demonstrations, marches and sit-ins, as they contradict Islamic Sharia law and the values and traditions of Saudi society," the interior ministry said. The country's council of senior clerics added: "The council ... affirms that demonstrations are forbidden in this country. The correct way in Sharia [law] of realising common interest is by advising, which is what the Prophet Muhammad established."

At the end of February 2011 the long oppressed Shia Muslim minority in the eastern province of Saudi Arabia began agitating for change. Many were arrested. The *Guardian* reported that up to 10,000 security forces were sent to the oil-rich area to quell the protests. Demonstrations in the Shia area continued intermittently throughout 2011 and in February 2012 at least six people were killed in the Qatif area of the eastern province. After these deaths the Saudi interior ministry released an ominous statement. "It is the state's right to confront those that confront it first... and the Saudi Arabian security forces will confront such situations... with determination and force and with an iron first."

Not a single one of the 200+ statements released by Foreign Affairs in 2011 concerned the repression in Saudi Arabia. The same can be said for the first eight months of 2012, after which this book went to print. Even when the monarchy targeted

76

Canadians the Conservatives generally stayed silent. For example, when Shaykh Usama Al-Atar led a group prayer in October 2011 the Edmonton-based Shia imam was beaten and arrested by police in Medina, but the Conservatives said little. "We were a bit surprised the Canadian government hasn't taken the role that it should and there's no support for him right now in Medina where he needs it most. He needs to be visited by consular officials," Massoud Shadjareh, spokesperson for the Islamic Human Rights Commission told CTV's *Canada AM*. After he was released from jail, Al-Atar, who was on a pilgrimage to Mecca, received a phone call from an embassy official in Riyadh. "I said to him, 'I expected you guys to be there sooner,' and his reply was that they couldn't find a plane to get them the 800 kilometres from Riyadh to Medina because it's the season of hajj," Al-Atar told the *Edmonton Journal*. "I was surprised at this answer, especially them being the Canadian government. I'm not sure how much effort was put into my release."

Al-Atar's experience reflects a pattern. The Conservatives refused to act when 21-year-old Nazia Quazi's father forced her to remain in Saudi Arabia by taking her Canadian and Indian passports as well as other identification. After being stuck in the country for two years Nazia asked the Saudi Human Rights Commission for help in December 2009 and, according to her account, was told "your father is doing all this for your own security, just respect that." With Canadian embassy officials unwilling to act, Human Rights Watch launched a campaign to put pressure on the Conservatives to issue Nazia a new passport and help her leave the country.

Nazia's case was similar to that of long-time Montréaler Nathalie Morin whose Saudi husband refused to let her and their three Canadian-born children leave the country. At one

point Morin was arrested by Saudi authorities when she left her apartment without her husband's permission. After three years Morin's husband agreed at the start of 2012 to let her return to Québec but Saudi officials refused to issue passports to her three children. Ottawa said little.

In January 2007 a 21 year-old Canadian studying in Saudi Arabia participated in an after-school brawl that left a 19-year-old dead. After a 90-minute trial (over several sessions) Mohamed Kohail and a Jordanian friend were sentenced to death by beheading. Kohail strenuously denied delivering the fatal blows in a fight that involved dozens of teenagers. Before the Conservatives took office Ottawa automatically lobbied foreign governments for mercy for Canadians facing the death penalty. Not the Conservatives. Ultimately, Kohail's death sentence was commuted but the Conservatives did little to help him.

In August 2010 the Saudis announced that they would ban Research in Motion's Blackberry services if the company refused to hand over access to its encrypted data transfer services. Unlike the previously mentioned individuals, the Conservatives immediately went to bat for the Waterloo-based company. But they did so in a positive manner, staying silent on the Saudis' flagrant censorship. In a bid to avert the ban, international trade minister Peter Van Loan called deputy interior minister Prince Mohammad Bin Naif Al Saud. "It was in the context of strengthening our relations that I called him concerning the operation of Research in Motion's BlackBerry services in Saudi Arabia," noted Van Loan. "I am pleased with the significant progress made in recent months in Canada-Saudi Arabia relations." According to unconfirmed press reports, the Canadian company ultimately agreed to place a BlackBerry server inside Saudi Arabia so the kingdom could

monitor messages as part of its policing of the internet for political content and obscenities.

What explains the Conservatives refusal to confront the Saudis? The answer is support for the monarchy's pro-US foreign policy as well as growing diplomatic, business and military relations between Canada and Saudi Arabia. Ministers Cannon, Van Loan, Baird, Ritz, Fast and Day (twice) visited Riyadh to meet the king or different Saudi princes. These trips spurred various business accords. According to the *Trade Lawyers Blog*, the Conservatives began discussing a Canada-Saudi Arabia foreign investment promotion and protection agreement in 2008. In February 2009 agriculture minister Gerry Ritz convinced Saudi Arabia to re-open its market to Canadian beef exporters and in October 2010 the two countries signed a memorandum of understanding to cooperate in health care. "This agreement will increase cooperation between our countries in health and medicine. It will create a positive environment for Canadian businesses to participate in major Saudi health care projects," said trade minister Van Loan during a visit to the country. About 10,000 Saudi government-sponsored students study in Canada, including 800 doctors and medical students pursuing graduate studies in Canada's hospitals and universities. Canada was added to the King Abdullah Scholarship Program in 2007. This program is generous to students and advantageous to Canadian universities which, according to a March 2010 *Globe and Mail* story, "benefit from pre-agreed research or bench fees to a university's faculty of graduate studies for [Saudi] master's and PhD students."

The Conservatives also developed military relations with the Saudis. For the first time, on January 10, 2010, *HMCS Fredericton* participated in a mobile refuelling exercise with a

Saudi military vessel. In another first, Saudi pilots began training in Moose Jaw, Saskatchewan and Cold Lake, Alberta in 2011 with NATO's Flying Training in Canada (NFTC). Dubbed "the benchmark for military flying training", NFTC is run by the Canadian Forces and Bombardier.

At the start of 2010 the government-backed Canadian Association of Defence and Security Industries sent its first-ever trade mission to Saudi Arabia. It was successful. According to a February 2012 Postmedia report, in 2011 the Conservatives approved arms export licences worth a whopping $4 billion to Saudi Arabia. Yet, by Ottawa's rules Canadian companies shouldn't sell weapons to the Saudis. Canada's export control policies, noted the Coalition to Oppose the Arms Trade, are supposed to "closely control" military exports to countries "involved in or under threat of hostilities" and countries "whose governments have a persistent record of serious violations of the human rights of their citizens." Despite these regulations, Saudi Arabia has been a leading purchaser of Canadian-made weaponry over the past two decades. During the first years of the Conservative government Canadian small arms, ammunition as well as various weapons systems and components, made their way to Saudi Arabia. From 2007-09, reported Project Ploughshares, Canada sold more than $4 million in goods grouped under ECL item 2-1, which corresponds most closely to the UN small arms category. But, Canada's main export to the Saudis was the wheels of war. A General Dynamics factory in London, Ontario produced more than 1,000 Light Armoured Vehicles (LAVs) for the Saudi military, who then used the vehicles (the production of which in Canada was subsidized by taxes) when they rolled into Bahrain. "The LAV-3 and other similar vehicles that Canada has supplied to the Saudi Arabian National Guard,"

noted Project Ploughshare's Ken Epps, "are exactly the kind of equipment that would be used to put down demonstrations [in Bahrain] and used against civilian populations."

Already equipped with hundreds of Canadian-built LAVs, the Saudis contracted General Dynamics Land Systems for another 724 LAVs in 2009. Since the vehicles were scheduled to be delivered weeks after the invasion of Bahrain, the Ottawa-based Rideau Institute called for a suspension of further arms shipments to the Saudis. The Conservatives ignored the call and as mentioned they approved $4 billion worth of arms exports in 2011, which included more (Canadian Commercial Corporation facilitated) LAVs.

But Canada didn't just sell the vehicles to Saudi Arabia. A Canadian colonel also led the General Dynamics Land Systems Saudi Arabian LAV support program. Mark E.K. Campbell has been in the army for more than three decades and, according to *Army.forces.gc.ca*, at the start of 2012 he sat on the Royal Canadian Regiment Association Museum Board and presided over the Western Ontario Branch of the Canadian Infantry Association.

In June 2010 the head of the Canadian Security Intelligence Service (CSIS), Richard Fadden, told the CBC that government officials were falling under the influence of foreign governments. Fadden made this statement a day before the Conservatives appointed an individual with ties to the Saudi monarchy to oversee CSIS. The government appointed former Québec health minister Philippe Couillard to the Security Intelligence Review Committee (SIRC), an agency that reports to Parliament on CSIS. SIRC officials have Level III clearance — the highest level — allowing them to access all top-secret material. Couillard was appointed to this sensitive position even though

he is paid by the Saudi health ministry to sit on its international advisory board. Couillard was quoted in the *National Post* saying his Saudi gig was "an important" part of his professional life. As part of his contract, Couillard travels to Riyadh at least once a year to meet the kingdom's health minister and according to the health ministry website Couillard represented its international advisory board at an April 2011 health insurance conference in Riyadh that included the Saudi health minister and a deputy minister.

Like most other Saudi institutions the health ministry has a repressive side. Some medical establishments have carried out amputations as judicial punishment and in 2010 a judge reportedly asked several hospitals if they would damage a man's spinal cord as a punishment. At least one hospital signalled its willingness to do so. Leaving aside these inhumane medical practices, would the Conservatives appoint an employee of much more free and democratic countries such as Bolivia, Cuba or Venezuela to a position where they could access top-secret Canadian documents? It's unlikely since the Conservatives don't consider the governments in those countries part of 'our team'. The Saudi leadership, however, is considered part of 'our team' so the Conservatives see no conflict with a person overseeing Canada's intelligence agency while working for the monarchy.

In a reflection of strong ties between the two countries' leaders, prominent Canadian institutions often work with the Saudis. When King Abdullah attended the 2010 G20 Summit in Toronto, he donated $5.33 million to the University of Toronto's Chair for Dialogue among Civilizations. Saudi Arabia finances a number of other educational and cultural initiatives in this country. Of most consequence, the royal family's Kingdom Holding Company and the Saudi Arabian Monetary Agency's Foreign

Holdings control substantial stock in a number of companies operating in Canada.

Most of the governments in the Saudi-led Gulf Cooperation Council (GCC) are major global investors, with many of the world's biggest sovereign wealth funds based there. According to the Foreign Affairs website: "The GCC is also a major source of foreign investment capital: by 2020, GCC countries are expected to have over US$3.5 trillion in foreign direct investment holdings." In a bid to entice investment in Canadian companies ministers Van Loan and Baird (as well as former prime ministers, turned corporate lobbyists, Brian Mulroney and Jean Chrétien) visited Prince Alwaleed, the head of Kingdom Holding Company. During the past few years Conservative ministers also visited officials from Qatar, the UAE and Kuwait to prod them to invest in Canadian businesses.

Claiming that more than $1 trillion would be spent on infrastructure projects in the region over the next several years, at the end of 2007 Export Development Canada, a crown corporation supporting foreign business ventures, established a GCC office. Ottawa also signed a Memorandum of Understanding on economic cooperation with the UAE and a foreign investment promotion and protection agreement with Kuwait. According to Foreign Affairs, "the Government of Canada has identified the GCC as a GCS [Global Commerce Strategy] priority market."

Alongside these diplomatic efforts Canada's trade and corporate presence in the region grew. The Royal Bank of Canada and the Bank of Montréal ramped up their operations in the GCC while Bombardier Transportation won $350 million in contracts to set up Monorail Systems in Riyadh and Jeddah. Simultaneously, the Montréal-based company launched a project management

academy to train managers in Saudi Arabia. During the past few years SNC-Lavalin has signed a number of contracts with state-owned oil company, Saudi Aramco. In July and August 2012 the Montréal-based company received $200 million in Saudi contracts and spent $40 million to acquire the industrial division of one of the country's largest industrial engineering groups.

Most significantly, the GCC is home to the only Tim Hortons outside of North America.

Business interests were only part of the Conservatives' growing ties to the GCC countries. There was also a geopolitical component to the relationship. A number of the GCC monarchies helped NATO attack Libya and they delivered weapons to the Sunni militias fighting the Assad dictatorship in Syria. In March 2012 minister Baird visited Doha to "gauge Qatar's perspective on the situation in Syria and the broader Middle East." During the same trip Baird said: "Saudi Arabia is an important player in the region and in the international community generally. We agreed on the need for united action to end the appalling violence in Syria perpetrated by the Assad regime." Two months later the foreign minister said "the UAE [is] ... a great political and military partner in Libya and politically on Syria."

The Sunni-Muslim GCC leadership considered Syria's Assad too close to Shia-led Hezbollah and Iran. Prodded by the US, the Gulf monarchies feared rising Iranian power and wanted to weaken the Hezbollah/Syria/Iran axis. For the Saudis, attacking the Alawite- (an offshoot of Shiasm) dominated Syrian regime was also a way to divide its internal opposition through sectarian politics. The Saudi leadership also supported the US-led campaign to contain Shia Iran. In March 2012 Baird said: "[Saudi] Prince Saud and I discussed our concerns regarding Iran's nuclear

program and its consistent refusal to abide by UN Security Council resolutions and allow full inspections by the International Atomic Energy Agency. We agreed that Iran is a destabilizing force in the region and that the international community has to remain united in its common interest of convincing the Iranian regime to reverse its current course and abandon any nuclear weapons program." Baird made a similar comment after meeting the royal families in Kuwait and the UAE. He told the January 2012 issue of *Diplomat and International Canada* that "throughout the Gulf and the Middle East there is deep concern about Iran's nuclear program."

Yet, surveys show that far fewer Arabs fear Iran than the US or Israel and most of the public is not particularly worried about the country's nuclear program. A 2010 Zogby International survey found that 88 percent of the region perceived Israel as a threat and 77 percent feared the US. Only 10 percent said the same of Iran and 77 percent of respondents agreed that Iran "has the right to its nuclear program." This poll was confirmed by a mid-2011 Doha Institute poll of 16,000 people in 12 Arab countries. Fifty-one percent of respondents named Israel as the leading threat to Arab national security while 22 percent cited the US. Only 5 percent of respondents pointed to Iran as the leading threat.

Baird's underlings at Foreign Affairs would, of course, be familiar with these polls. But popular attitudes are irrelevant to the Conservatives. They care about the ruling monarchies' position, which Baird defines as "throughout the Gulf and the Middle East." His comment demonstrates the Conservatives' utter contempt for the democratic will of ordinary people across the Arab world. But of course this attitude towards the concerns of anyone who is not part of the elite is a consistent theme when describing Harper's foreign policy around the world.

4. Bombing Libya

While Canada's foreign policy under Harper has consistently demonstrated contempt for the concerns of ordinary people, on a few occasions it has veered into outright militaristic bullying. One of those occasions was during Canada's participation in the bombing of a small North African country.

A few days after Mubarak was driven from power in Egypt major protests began in eastern Libya. On February 15, 2011, up to 500 demonstrated in Benghazi against Muammar Gaddafi's 42-year rule. Dozens were injured when the police dispersed the protest. Over the following days demonstrators took to the streets in a number of protests that quickly turned violent. Scores of demonstrators calling for an end to Gaddafi's rule were killed. On the other hand, numerous government officials were also killed. The conflict quickly descended into a civil war.

Though they were largely indifferent to the state-backed killing in Tunisia and Egypt, the Conservatives quickly denounced Gaddafi's repression. On February 21 foreign minister Cannon "strongly condemned the violent crackdowns on innocent demonstrators." That same day Harper added: "We find the actions of the government, firing upon its own citizens, to be outrageous and unacceptable and we call on the government to cease that kind of violence immediately." A few days later Conservative officials called on Gaddafi to step down. Cannon said: "It is clear that the only acceptable course of action for Gaddafi is to halt the bloodshed and to immediately vacate his position and authority." Conspicuously avoiding the protests then taking place against Western-backed dictators in Jordan, Saudi Arabia, Yemen, Bahrain, Morocco etc.,

on February 28 Cannon told the UN Human Rights Council in Geneva: "A tide of change is sweeping the Middle East and North Africa. Leaders who try to defy or repress the tide, like Gaddafi or the leadership in Iran, will eventually be overwhelmed." (At that time there weren't any major demonstrations in Iran.)

It was easy for Western governments to criticize the Libyan crackdown since Gaddafi was never their preferred leader (though in 2011 the Libyan leader was on better terms with the West than in the 1980s). Widely derided for supporting Mubarak to the bitter end, criticizing Gaddafi gave Harper an opportunity to re-affirm his "principled" foreign policy rhetoric. Another reason for the intervention (see below for greater detail) was the timing of the Libyan protests and the country's geographic location. Influencing developments in Libya gave the West another point of leverage over the revolutions in bordering Tunisia and Egypt. The intervention demonstrated to the Arab world that Western powers were prepared to use force to assert their interests. This happened at the same time as they tacitly supported the Saudi invasion of Bahrain. In ramping up the war drums, the Western alliance diverted international attention from the repression of protesters in the more geopolitically sensitive Gulf region.

On February 26 the United Nations Security Council (UNSC) passed resolution 1970 calling for an arms embargo of Libya as well as a travel ban and asset freeze on leaders of the Libyan regime. The Conservatives immediately went beyond UNSCR 1970, freezing all of Libya's assets in Canada and blocking financial transactions with the country's government or institutions. In contrast, during the weeks before Mubarak and Ben Ali were driven from office the Conservatives failed to implement sanctions against Egypt or Tunisia.

Then, three weeks before Parliament and the UN approved the Libyan intervention, the Conservatives began a military campaign. On February 28 *CTV.ca* reported "that Canadian special forces are also on the ground in Libya." Two days later, 15 days before the Security Council authorized a no-fly zone, Navy frigate *HMCS Charlottetown* left Halifax for Libya. In a March 1 *Globe and Mail* article titled "Canada girds for substantial military role in North Africa" defence minister Peter MacKay explained the objective of the naval deployment. "We are there for all inevitabilities. And NATO is looking at this as well ... This is taken as a precautionary and staged measure."

Though not a member of the Security Council, Ottawa backed a no-fly zone over Libya, which US Defense Secretary Robert Gates and many others considered an act of war. "A no-fly zone", Gates told Congress a week before the UN vote, "begins with an attack on Libya to destroy the air defenses." With China, Russia, Germany, Brazil and Turkey abstaining, on March 17 the UNSC backed a plan to implement a no-fly zone over Libya. Immediately after UNSCR 1973 passed, Harper left for a summit in Paris to plot the military campaign and foreign minister Cannon claimed UNSCR 1973 allowed "boots on the ground".

As the France/US/UK/Qatar/Canada coalition excitedly hurried towards war others tried to broker a cease-fire and political negotiations between Gaddafi and the rebels. On March 10 the International Crisis Group (ICG), a leading non-profit, called for a committee of Libya's North African neighbours and other African states to broker a ceasefire and negotiations between the rebels and Gaddafi. The ICG's aim was to replace the regime with a more representative and law-abiding government and its proposal included a provision for a UN peacekeeping force to secure a

ceasefire. The ICG's plan was broadly in line with the position of the African Union, Russia, China, Brazil and India as well as Germany and Turkey. Six days after their initial statement, on the eve of the debate that led to UNSCR 1973, the ICG submitted a more detailed proposal to protect civilians and move towards a more legitimate government. Unconvinced by the ICG and other countries, the powerbrokers in Washington, London, Paris and Ottawa chose war before pursuing other options.

The day after UNSCR 1973 passed, Gaddafi's forces on the southern edge of Benghazi announced a ceasefire as per Article 1 of the UN resolution and they proposed a political dialogue in conformity with Article 2. This ceasefire was immediately rejected by senior rebel commander Khalifa Haftar and dismissed by Western governments. US president Obama called on Gaddafi to withdraw his forces from Benghazi and Misrata as well as Ajdabiya and Zawiya, the main towns his troops had retaken from the rebels — and to sustain the ceasefire, single-handedly, irrespective of the rebels. Basically, Obama called on Gaddafi to accept strategic defeat in advance of negotiations, a position absent from UNSCR 1973.

Gaddafi's first ceasefire as well as subsequent offers on March 20, April 30, May 26 and June 9 were rejected or ignored. At the end of March Turkey announced that it was talking to both sides, but its offer to broker a ceasefire was ignored. Though his country is a member of NATO, early in the intervention Turkish president Recep Erdogan criticized the bombing campaign. "I wish that those who only see oil, gold mines and underground treasures when they look in [Libya's] direction, would see the region through glasses of conscience from now on." During the second week of April the African Union pursued a ceasefire, which

was immediately rejected by the rebels' National Transitional Council (NTC). The rebels, explained Libya expert Hugh Roberts, "demanded Gaddafi's resignation as a condition of any ceasefire a demand that made a ceasefire impossible, since securing a ceasefire requires commanders with decisive authority over their armies, and removing Gaddafi would have meant that no one any longer had overall authority over the regime's forces."

Three months into the intervention the International Crisis Group complained that NATO and the NTC rejected all peace initiatives. "UNSC resolution 1973 emphatically called for a ceasefire, yet every proposal for a ceasefire put forward by the Gaddafi regime or by third parties so far has been rejected by the NTC as well as by the Western governments most closely associated with the NATO military campaign... neither the NTC nor NATO has made a ceasefire proposal of its own and there has yet to be a meaningful attempt to test Gaddafi's seriousness or pose conditions on acceptance that would subject a putative ceasefire to effective independent supervision."

Briefing notes uncovered by the *Ottawa Citizen* show that foreign minister Baird pushed the NTC to keep fighting when he visited Benghazi in June 2011. "Hawkish Baird urged Libyan rebels to keep up fight", noted an April 2012 headline describing the minister's visit with the rebels three months into the conflict. In public he called for an end to the fighting, but in private Baird "impressed upon the National Transitional Council the importance of pushing forward militarily."

From March to October 2011 an alliance of mostly NATO nations waged war in Libya. Begun under the pretext of saving civilians from Gaddafi's terror, the real aim was regime change. The UN "no-fly zone" immediately became a license to

bomb Libyan tanks, government installations and other targets in coordination with rebel attacks. NATO also bombed Gaddafi's compound and the houses of people close to him. The military alliance defined "effective protection" of civilians as per UNSCR 1973, noted Hugh Roberts, as "requir[ing] the elimination of the threat, which was Gaddafi himself for as long as he was in power (subsequently revised to 'for as long as he is in Libya' before finally becoming 'for as long as he is alive')."

Early in the bombing campaign Harper suggested the goal was to force Gaddafi out. On March 19 he said: "It is our belief that if Mr. Gaddafi loses the capacity to enforce his will through vastly superior armed forces, he simply will not be able to sustain his grip on the country." The prime minister later celebrated the dictator's summary execution. "Harper hails Gaddafi's death", noted a *Globe and Mail* headline. Apparently, the Conservatives wanted to make sure Gaddafi was taken out by force. In April 2012 *La Presse* reported on internal documents that showed how Ottawa pressed neighbouring countries not to grant Gaddafi exile after Tripoli fell. A September 2011 document explained: "There is a fear that Gaddafi is seeking asylum and assistance of neighbouring countries that have maintained good relations with Libya. ... A study on the options available to Canada to influence these countries to refrain from providing any aid or safe haven to Gaddafi was also conducted."

The Canadian Forces played an important part in the coalition that waged war on Libya. Two thousand Canadian soldiers participated in the war and a Canadian general led the campaign. Charles Bouchard commanded the entire operation "personally sign[ing] off on every last preselected [bombing] target," according to the *Globe and Mail*.

Bouchard took a particularly belligerent tone. Three months into the war, on June 22, a leading member of the coalition, Italy, called for a ceasefire to deliver aid. Foreign minister Franco Frattini said "I believe an immediate humanitarian suspension of hostilities is required in order to create effective humanitarian corridors." The Canadian commander, who later received a Canadian and US medal of honour, dismissed this out of hand. "A ceasefire, temporary in nature, cannot be just an opportunity for both sides to reload and to engage in further violence down the road," Bouchard declared. "We must continue to stay engaged to prevent that rearming and reinforcement from taking place." The Canadian general went on to say "Gaddafi is hiding in hospitals, hiding in mosques, he's hiding under various covers everywhere. He is keeping well clear of command and control nodes."

The Italians were partly concerned about the growing number of civilian casualties. On June 20 as many as 19 people, including eight children, were reportedly killed by a coalition strike at the home of a top Gaddafi official 70 km west of Tripoli. A day earlier NATO admitted they hit a house in Tripoli, killing a number of civilians.

Fifteen Canadian aircraft participated in the war. Using 14.5 million pounds of fuel during the fighting, the Canadian air force was responsible for 10 percent of all coalition sorties, or some 1,500 missions. Only the US, France, Britain and Italy contributed more to the air war. And numbers don't reveal the full extent of Canada's role. A number of coalition members, including Turkey, Sweden, the UAE and Qatar, placed strict restrictions on their forces' ability to strike ground targets. These and other countries' militaries frequently "red carded" sorties, declaring that they would not contribute. "With a Canadian general in charge,"

explained the *Globe and Mail*, "Canada couldn't have red-carded missions even if it wanted to, which is why Canadian CF-18 pilots often found themselves in the most dangerous skies" doing the dirtiest work.

Not much is known about their operation since the Canadian Forces was less forthcoming with details than some other coalition members. "CF [Canadian Forces] spokesman Brig. Gen. Richard Blanchette," noted the *Ottawa Citizen*'s David Pugliese, "claims that detailing the type or numbers of bombs dropped on targets (or even naming specific targets) would violate operational security."

Nevertheless, some information did trickle out. *CBC.ca* reported that on March 29, 2011, two CF-18s launched strikes that directly aided the rebels in Misrata and on May 19 Canadian jets participated in a mission that destroyed eight Libyan naval vessels. On their return to Canada, *CBC.ca* reported: "[pilot Maj. Yves] Leblanc's crew carried out the final mission on the day Gaddafi was captured, and were flying 25,000 feet over when Gaddafi's convoy was attacked." Human Rights Watch found the remains of at least 95 people at the site where Muammar Gaddafi was captured. According to the human rights group, "the vast majority had apparently died in the fighting and NATO strikes prior to Gaddafi's capture" with another six to ten apparently executed by close range gunshot wounds. Some accused NATO forces of helping to murder Gaddafi.

Seven Canadian CF-18 fighter jets dropped at least 700 bombs on Libyan targets. Two months into the bombing United Press International reported that Ottawa "ordered 1,300 replacement laser-guided bombs to use in its NATO mission in Libya" and a month later they ordered another 1,000 bomb kits.

Two Canadian CP-140 Aurora spy planes, with multimillion dollar sensors, participated in the war. They intercepted Libyan communications and waged psychological war, dropping anti-Gaddafi leaflets and broadcasting critical radio transmissions, which the Libyan government tried to jam. According to a Canadian Press article, "Canadian CP-140 Aurora surveillance planes recently started broadcasting propaganda messages aimed at forces loyal to Libyan strongman Muammar Gaddafi."

From high in the sky to the country's coastal plains, the Canadian Forces engaged in combat. On September 13, three weeks after Tripoli fell, Canada's state broadcaster reported: "CBC News has learned there are members of the Canadian Forces on the ground in Libya." A number of media outlets reported that highly secretive Canadian special forces were fighting in Libya. As mentioned earlier, on February 28, *CTV.ca* reported "that Canadian special forces are also on the ground in Libya" while *Esprit du Corp* editor Scott Taylor noted Canadian Special Operations Regiment's flag colours in the Conservatives' post-war celebration. But, notwithstanding minister Cannon's proclamation, any Canadian "boots on the ground" in Libya violated UNSCR 1973. The resolution explicitly excluded "a foreign occupation force of any form on any part of Libyan territory."

Few details about Canadian special forces activities in Libya have become public, but presumably they engaged alongside allied British, US and French special forces as well as those from Qatar and Jordan. (Journalists in Libya during the conflict repeatedly spotted armed Westerners who appeared to be special forces or former soldiers employed by private companies.) On March 30 the *New York Times* reported: "Former British officials said that dozens of British Special Forces and MI6 intelligence

officers are working inside Libya. The British operatives have been directing airstrikes by British jets and gathering intelligence about the whereabouts of Libyan government tank columns, artillery pieces and missile installations." The paper added that American officials admitted that "small groups of C.I.A. operatives have been working in Libya for several weeks as part of a shadow force of Westerners that the Obama administration hopes can help bleed Colonel Gaddafi's military."

After the conclusion of hostilities a number of stories detailed the British and Qatari special forces role in Libya. According to a BBC report titled *Inside story of the UK's secret mission to beat Gaddafi*, British special forces were "co-ordinating certain NATO air attacks." For example, during the rebel attack against "Gaddafi's home town of Sirte, they were assisted by a handful of British and other special forces."

Two rotations of Canadian warships enforced a naval blockade of Libya with about 250 soldiers aboard each vessel. On May 19 *HMCS Charlottetown* participated in an operation that destroyed eight Libyan naval vessels. The ship also repelled a number of fast, small boats and escaped unscathed when a dozen missiles were fired towards it from the port city of Misrata. After the hostilities the head of Canada's navy, Paul Maddison, told Ottawa defence contractors that *HMCS Charlottetown* "played a key role in keeping the Port of Misrata open as a critical enabler of the anti-Gaddafi forces." On one occasion a Canadian warship, part of a 20-ship NATO flotilla supposedly enforcing the UN arms embargo on Libya, boarded a rebel vessel full of weapons. "There are loads of weapons and munitions, more than I thought," a Canadian officer radioed *HMCS Charlottetown* commander Craig Skjerpen. "From small ammunition to 105 howitzer rounds

and lots of explosives." The commander's response, reported the *Ottawa Citizen*, was to allow the rebel ship to sail through.

In fact, the Canadian government directly armed the rebels. In contravention of international law, Waterloo-based Aeryon Scout Micro supplied the rebels with a three-pound, backpack-sized Unmanned Aerial Vehicle. The director of field support for the company, Charles Barlow, traveled 18 hours on a rebel operated boat from Malta to the NTC training facility in Misrata. There, Barlow taught the rebels how to operate this Canadian-developed drone, which was used to gather intelligence on the front lines. In an interview after Gaddafi's death, Barlow said: "I hope we did a little tiny part to help get rid of that man."

According to various reports the drone was paid for out of Libyan government assets frozen in Canada. Aeryon CEO Dave Kroetsch said the company was "approached by the Canadian government." But, in April Foreign Affairs officials advised minister Cannon that providing military assistance to the Libyan rebels contravened UNSCR 1970. Based on documents uncovered through the Access to Information Act, Project Ploughshares reported: "A 'Memorandum for Action' signed by the Minister on April 11, noted that under the UN Security Council resolution that established the arms embargo against Libya, 'Canada generally cannot permit the export of arms to Libya without the prior approval of the UN 1970 Sanctions Committee.' The memo also stated that the arms embargo 'encompasses any type of weapon ... as well as technical assistance such as the provision of instruction, training or intelligence.' It confirms that the UN arms embargo on Libya precluded the transfer of the Canadian surveillance drone to Libyan opposition forces. However, the memo also provided an interpretive feint for Canada by which it could allow the drone

to be exported. It noted that Security Council Resolution 1973 contains language that key partners the US, the UK and France interpreted as permitting provision of arms to Libyan opposition forces as part of 'all necessary measures ... to protect civilians.' The memo was clear that this interpretation was not shared by many other states, including NATO allies Italy and Norway."

The government failed to inform all departments about its interpretive feint. In early 2012 a Canadian Forces website plainly stated that UNSCR 1970 "called for an international arms embargo on Libya" and "[UNSCR] 1973 of 17 March, which strengthened the arms embargo."

On top of sending weapons, troops and advisers some NATO members and Arab countries of the Libya Contact Group established a fund to assist the rebels. The money mostly came from the hundred billion dollars in Libyan government assets seized around the world. "Canada mulls ways to fund Libyan rebels with [$2.2 billion in] frozen Gaddafi assets," noted a *Globe and Mail* headline. In an unprecedented move, the anti-Gaddafi coalition used Libyan government assets to unseat the Libyan government. While a number of allies immediately released funds to the NTC, Canadian law requires the government to follow Security Council sanctions, which delayed releasing funds. Publicly, Baird said: "We don't have the capacity to turn over the Libyan people's resources to the legitimate representative [NTC]." There was talk of providing the NTC with a line of credit and using the frozen assets as collateral. It's not clear if the Conservatives did so, but as noted above, some press reports claimed the Canadian drone sold to the rebels was paid for with those frozen assets. Finally, in mid-September Ottawa secured an exemption from the Security Council's sanctions committee to officially unfreeze Libyan assets.

As part of the legal process of distributing frozen Libyan assets to the rebels, on June 14 Canada recognized the NTC as the legitimate voice of the country's people even though the rebels controlled no more than a sliver of the country's territory. Two weeks later John Baird secretly flew to rebel-held Benghazi in his first overseas trip as foreign minister. Calling the NTC the "best hope" for Libya, Baird said: "Obviously no government can be worse than the Gaddafi regime. I think we need to be realistic. We're not going to move from Gaddafi to Thomas Jefferson overnight." On top of urging the rebels to keep fighting, on this trip Baird visited the NATO command in Naples where he wrote on a bomb: "Free Libya. Democracy". It is not known if anyone in Libya managed to read the message before the bomb exploded on their country.

After the Libyan leader was killed Baird was the first foreign minister to visit Gaddafi's Tripoli compound. Canada was also among the first countries to re-open its embassy in Tripoli. And as usual, when Canadian or US troops intervene in another country, a significant amount of Canadian "aid" money was quickly delivered to Libya. Ottawa first announced $10 million in aid and then as the conflict wound down Foreign Affairs gave the NTC another "$10 million to help secure weapons of mass destruction and remove and dispose of explosive remnants of war." On June 14 Canada gave $1.75 million to the International Committee of the Red Cross as well as $250,000 to the Red Crescent Society "to protect women and girls from gender-based violence—including sexual assault—and provide critical care to survivors in Libya." A number of Foreign Affairs press releases cited this aid disbursement. One described "an additional $2 million in humanitarian assistance to respond to the needs of conflict-affected populations, including

survivors of sexual violence" while another mentioned "$2 million in … dedicated funding to assist victims of rape—which is being widely used as a weapon of war in the conflict."

Devoting funds to combating gender-based violence is usually a worthy cause but in this case it was part of an attempt to justify NATO's intervention. The rebels accused Gaddafi's forces of mass rape, a charge that was repeated by Western media and politicians. According to the *Guardian*, "tales of raping sprees by sub-Saharan African mercenaries — fuelled in one version by Viagra doled out by Gaddafi — abound in Libya." Incredibly, the US ambassador to the UN, Susan Rice, cited the obviously outlandish (and racist) Viagra allegation at a closed session of the international body. Canadian foreign minister Baird was still repeating the mass rape justification for bombing Libya months after Gaddafi was killed. At the end of 2011 he told CTV: "When you talk about rape as an instrument of war, women being raped in Libya, it's a very uncomfortable issue. Just ignoring it, throwing it under the carpet, it's not an option."

But did Gaddafi's forces engage in mass rape? Probably not, according to experienced human rights investigators. Amnesty International's senior crisis response adviser Donatella Rovera, who was in Libya for three months after the start of the uprising, said: "We have not found any evidence or a single victim of rape or a doctor who knew about somebody being raped." Liesel Gerntholtz, head of women's rights at Human Rights Watch, concurred. "We have not been able to find evidence [of mass rape]." According to a June 24 report in the London *Independent*, Amnesty's specialist on Libya, Diana Eltahawy, met the most reputable source for the mass rape claim. Libyan psychologist, Seham Sergewa, said she distributed 70,000 questionnaires in rebel-controlled areas

and along the Tunisian border. The psychologist claimed 60,000 were returned with 259 women volunteering that they were raped. According to Sergewa's account, she then interviewed 140 of the victims. Yet when Amnesty's Libya specialist asked to meet some of the women Sergewa said "she had lost contact with them" and could not provide documentary evidence.

Amnesty and Human Rights Watch's lack of documentary evidence does not, of course, conclusively disprove that rape was employed by Gaddafi's forces. It does suggest, however, that the rebels (at minimum) exaggerated the claim, which would fit within a long established history of lying during war.

One of the main incidents that justified the intervention was the claim that on February 21, 2011, Libyan helicopters and fighter jets fired and dropped bombs on civilians. Without any video proof Qatar's *Al Jazeera* broadcast these accusations, which were picked up by much of the Western media. Some even talked of genocide. During a high profile post-war celebration Harper repeated a variation of this claim. "The Gaddafi regime responded, unleashing the full fury of the state — police, army and air force — against them, calling all who protested 'germs, rats, scumbags and cockroaches,' and demanded Libya be cleansed 'house by house'. It was an invitation to genocide."

But, what's the evidence for this accusation? Researchers from both the International Crisis Group (ICG) and Amnesty couldn't find any evidence that Gaddafi's forces fired on civilians from fighter jets or helicopters. In June 2011 the ICG explained: "There are grounds for questioning the more sensational reports that the regime was using its air force to slaughter demonstrators, let alone engaging in anything remotely warranting use of the term 'genocide'." In a *London Review of Books* article after the conflict

ICG researcher Hugh Roberts wrote: "In the days that followed I made efforts to check the *Al-Jazeera* story." But none of the news items provided any "corroboration ... that Gaddafi's fighter jets (or any other aircraft) had strafed or bombed anyone in Tripoli or anywhere else... I was in Egypt for most of the time, but since many journalists visiting Libya were transiting through Cairo, I made a point of asking those I could get hold of what they had picked up in the field. None of them had found any corroboration of the story." Similarly, on March 2, 2011, US Defense Secretary Robert Gates and Admiral Mike Mullen, chairman of the Joint Chiefs of Staff, told Congress they couldn't confirm the reports of aircraft controlled by Gaddafi loyalists firing on civilians.

After three months in rebel-controlled territory Amnesty's investigator confirmed between 100 and 110 deaths in Benghazi and 59 to 64 in Baida (these totals include some presumed Gaddafi supporters). While this is an appalling level of state violence, it's much fewer than the thousands, even ten thousand, mentioned to justify the no fly zone. At the time even some mainstream voices suggested the Libyan opposition was exaggerating. A March 22, 2011, *USA Today* op-ed explained: "Despite ubiquitous cellphone cameras, there are no images of genocidal violence, a claim that smacks of rebel propaganda."

Another justification for the Western intervention was that Gaddafi used mercenaries to repress his people. "Unconfirmed reports," noted the *Guardian* only four days after the first signs of protest, "claim that [a Khamis Gaddafi led] force has been backed by African mercenaries brought into the country in five separate flights."

International researchers found very limited evidence supporting this claim. The UN Report of the International

102

Commission of Inquiry on Libya dismissed it and so did Amnesty. The human rights group explained: "We examined this issue in depth and found no evidence. The rebels spread these rumours everywhere, which had terrible consequences for African guest workers: there was a systematic hunt for migrants, some were lynched and many arrested. Since then, even the rebels have admitted there were no mercenaries, almost all have been released and have returned to their countries of origin, as the investigations into them revealed nothing."

The claim that Gaddafi relied on mercenaries was particularly useful to the western alliance as it implied that he was both brutal and little supported. But, it's clear from the length of the war, as well as a number of major pro-government demonstrations, that Gaddafi enjoyed substantial support (as did the NTC in parts of the country). Even with NATO's support it took the NTC five months to take Tripoli. Once the capital was lost, Gaddafi's forces hung on for another month in Bani Walid and then a further month in Sirte.

Ultimately Gaddafi's forces were no match for "NATO's military strategy in Libya." Three months into the conflict the *Globe and Mail* described that strategy as "to press on, keep firing, until the people of Tripoli rise up against Muammar Gaddafi." The Canadian commander in charge of the mission was relatively open about the plan. "Our point is to degrade the forces to stop them from using violence," Charles Bouchard said three months into the conflict. "But at the end of the day, the population itself will have to make that choice to uprise [rise up]." After Gaddafi was killed, a Canadian air force officer, Kirk 'Rambo' Soroka, told *Canadian Business* "We wrote the air campaign plan [at NATO's Crisis Action Branch in Italy] ... I focused on two lines of operation:

how to defeat the enemy economically and how to defeat him operationally." The alliance, reported the *Ottawa Citizen* in February 2012, dropped 20,000 bombs on almost 6,000 targets, including more than 400 government buildings or command centres, in pursuit of this strategy.

The human toll of NATO's war strategy was not insignificant. Human Rights Watch found that the air strikes killed no less than 72 civilians. An investigation by three Middle Eastern human rights groups found evidence that all sides, including NATO, committed war crimes. Sponsored by the Arab Organisation for Human Rights, the Palestinian Centre for Human Rights and the International Legal Assistance Consortium, the Independent Civil Society Mission to Libya found evidence that NATO erroneously classified some civilian sites they struck as military targets. Raji Sourani, head of the Palestinian Centre for Human Rights, said: "We are asking questions, especially about what happened in Sirte" where NATO apparently killed 47 civilians in one strike. Eyewitnesses told the Independent Civil Society Mission to Libya that civilians converged on two trucks destroyed by NATO airplanes and were struck by a third NATO missile.

It's not clear how many died in fighting between Gaddafi's forces and rebels, which may have been extended by the outside intervention. *Guardian* columnist Seumas Milne explained: "While the death toll in Libya when NATO intervened was perhaps around 1,000-2,000 (judging by UN estimates), eight months later it is probably more than ten times that figure." He added: "If the purpose of western intervention in Libya's civil war was to 'protect civilians' and save lives, it has been a catastrophic failure."

Those pushing for intervention made bold predictions about what Gaddafi's forces would do if they captured Benghazi.

For the most part, however, they were uninterested in what actually happened when the NTC won. Gaddafi's final stronghold, Sirte, was the site of widespread war crimes. Under siege by NATO fighter jets, this city of 100,000 was cut off from outside water, medicine, food and electricity supplies for weeks. After they captured the city the rebels executed hundreds. *CBSnews.com* reported: "Nearly 300 bodies, many of them with their hands tied behind their backs and shot in the head, have been collected from across Sirte and buried in a mass grave. ... There are no names in one graveyard, only numbers: 572 so far and counting."

Human Rights Watch found an "apparent execution of 53 Gaddafi supporters" at one site. "We found 53 decomposing bodies, apparently Gaddafi supporters, at an abandoned hotel in Sirte, and some had their hands bound behind their backs when they were shot," reported Peter Bouckaert, emergencies director at Human Rights Watch. Bouckaert further explained: "This latest massacre seems part of a trend of killings, looting, and other abuses committed by armed anti-Gaddafi fighters who consider themselves above the law."

At the start of 2012 UN human rights chief Navi Pillay said militia groups held more than 8,500 detainees, mostly Gaddafi loyalists, in 60 different locations. Four months after Tripoli fell Doctors Without Borders withdrew from Misrata because of rampant prisoner torture. "Our role is to provide medical care to war casualties and sick detainees, not to repeatedly treat the same patients between torture sessions," said Doctors Without Borders general director Christopher Stokes. In February 2012 Peter Bouckaert said: "People are turning up dead in detention at an alarming rate... If this was happening under any Arab dictatorship, there would be an outcry."

Amnesty reported "black Libyans and sub-Saharan Africans are at high risk of abuse by anti-Gaddafi forces" while a Turkish construction contractor told the BBC that he saw 70 Chadians who worked for his company killed. A largely black town just outside of Misrata was entirely emptied of its 30,000 residents. Tawarga became a "closed military area" according to the rebels. Two weeks after Tripoli fell *Antiwar.com*'s Jason Ditz explained: "Black people have been disappearing all across Libya, with rebels arresting people simply on the basis of skin colour, but how does a whole city go missing? It may be quite some time before we learn exactly what happened, but we have hints in media reports dating back to June, when Misrata rebels began openly talking about 'cleansing' the region of blacks and were saying that black Libyans might as well pack up because 'Tawarga no longer exists, only Misrata.'"

At the start of 2012 the Canadian commander of the NATO mission told a senate committee meeting he was aware that the "fate of the individuals of Tawarga continues." But, according to the *Ottawa Citizen*, General Bouchard added: "Many of these individuals are still remnants of mercenaries who need to move out of the country and need to go home because there is no value in keeping them."

Eight months after the end of the conflict, in May 2012, the NTC introduced a series of repressive laws. After giving everyone who fought against Gaddafi's regime a blanket amnesty, they made it illegal — punishable by life in prison — to glorify any aspect of Gaddafi's 40-year reign. The same punishment awaited anyone who "attacks the February 17 revolution, denigrates Islam, the authority of the state or its institutions." Human Rights Watch pointed out that this law was similar to Gaddafi's rule

banning criticism. It was one of many repressive tactics the new government borrowed from the former regime. In July 2012 the *Wall Street Journal* reported: "Libya's caretaker government has quietly reactivated some of the interception equipment that fallen dictator Muammar Gaddafi once used to spy on his opponents. The surveillance equipment has been used in recent months to track the phone calls and online communications of Gaddafi loyalists."

In addition to intensifying the conflict and making foreigners the arbiters of Libyan politics, the Western war reinforced the idea that the traditional imperial powers have the right to intervene militarily in southern countries' affairs. The intervention and UNSCR 1973 further undermined respect for state sovereignty, which provides the weakest states with some protection from the most powerful. Many Africans, Asians and Latin Americans opposed the intervention precisely because they feared that it would establish a precedent that might lead to their country's sovereignty being violated. In fact, one reason the NATO powers intervened in Libya was to reassert their 'right' to do so. With Gaddafi widely demonized before his forces attacked protesters in the East it was easy for Ottawa/Paris/London/Washington to justify the Libyan mission.

Beyond reasserting this 'right', the Libyan mission strengthened NATO, the Western alliance's main interventionist body. Defence minister McKay explained: "Clearly with Afghanistan still on everyone's horizon, with the [Kosovo] mission, other challenges in places like Africa, Libya stands out as one of those missions that has truly reinforced the raison d'etre for NATO." For his part, British defence chief, David Richards, called the Libyan mission "one of the most successful operations NATO has conducted in its 62-year history."

The military mission also strengthened the Canadian Forces. The government and military immediately embraced the fighting in Libya. Harper described Canada's initial flyovers as "acts of war" and to get us in the fighting spirit the military released onboard video footage of a CF-18 destroying a Libyan ground target. After the war the Conservatives spent $850,000 on a nationally televised war celebration for the troops that fought in Libya. Harper called it "a day of honour … Soldier for soldier, sailor for sailor, airman for airman, the Canadian Armed Forces are the best in the world." For Harper — and other Western leaders — the intervention was an opportunity to test weaponry against a weak opponent. The military doesn't buy weapons simply for the sake of it. The head of the army, Lieutenant-General Andrew Leslie, pointed this out in 2007: "Let's not kid ourselves, the resources are not for Afghanistan alone. In the near future, we'll be going somewhere similar to Afghanistan, doing the same sorts of things."

The conflict in Libya came at an opportune time for the Conservatives. Their supporters used it to justify spending tens of billions of dollars on 65 F-35 fighter jets, which was a serious political headache that should have cost the Conservatives during the 2011 election campaign. A Nanos poll released days before the intervention (and only weeks prior to the election) found that 68 percent of Canadians — including a majority of Conservative supporters — agreed that "now is not a good time" to spend billions of dollars on these single-engine jets. Sending Canadian military aircraft to enforce a UN "no-fly zone" in Libya provided an opportunity to soften opposition to the F-35 purchase. The right-wing press immediately connected the dots. An *Ottawa Citizen* headline read: "Libya shows why Canada needs [F-35] jets" and a Sun Media chain commentary explained: "enforcing a 'no-

fly' zone to shut down a dictator is an expeditionary air operation. Is that something Canadians want to be able to do in the future? If yes, you need an F-35, expensive or not." Prime Minister Harper defended the plan to buy F-35s by saying: "You know, the CF-18s that are flying over Libya right now, they will come to the end of their useful life in the next few years." Most critics of the F-35 purchase supported the 'humanitarian' mission in Libya. With the opposition parties (minus Green MP Elizabeth May) supporting the bombing campaign, Harper was able to deflect criticism about spending $1,000 per Canadian on the best fighter jets money can buy. (Québec housing group FRAPRU claimed the cost of a single F-35 equals 6,400 social housing units.)

But like most wars, the Libya campaign also had economic roots. Two days after the bombing began the *Financial Times* reported that Western oil companies were worried that if Gaddafi defeated the rebels he would nationalize their operations out of anger at the West's duplicity. Presumably, this included Suncor, Canada's second largest corporation, which signed a multi-billion dollar 30-year oil concession with Libya in 2008. Home to the second largest amount of Canadian investment in Africa, instability in Libya put a couple billion dollars of this country's corporate investment in jeopardy. Dru Oja Jay, editor of *The Dominion*, noted: "Canadian investors are legitimately worried about what's going to happen to the $1 billion signing bonus Suncor paid out to the Libyan government, or whether SNC Lavalin is going to recoup its investments in the country, which is home to 10% of its workforce." Would a victorious Gaddafi have moved against Canadian companies? Even if he didn't, with all the bad press SNC and Suncor received could they have continued in Libya without regime change?

After the conflict the Conservatives expressed concern about the investments disrupted by the invasion. "How do we make sure that Canadian companies who have half-finished projects can get in there and finish them?" asked Baird in an end of 2011 interview with *Diplomat and International Canada*. Significant sums of Canadian investment would have been in jeopardy had Gaddafi defeated the rebellion and reasserted his authority. Milder criticism than that which the Conservatives directed against Gaddafi at the start of the conflict had previously led the Libyan dictator to penalize Canadian corporations. In September 2009 the Libyan leader's plane was set to land in St. John's to refuel. Foreign minister Cannon, who planned to meet Gaddafi on his stop-over in Newfoundland, announced that he would rebuke the Libyan dictator for giving the Lockerbie bomber, Abdel Basset al-Megrahi, a "hero's welcome" when he was released from a Scottish jail weeks earlier. The planned refuelling and Cannon's criticism garnered significant media attention and caused Gaddafi to cancel the stopover. Moreover the bad blood cost Suncor. An October 2009 cable from the US Embassy in Tripoli, released by Wikileaks, titled "PETROCANADA [Suncor] CAUGHT IN GADDAFI'S CROSS-HAIRS" explained: "the Libyan government demanded PetroCanada cut its oil production due to misunderstandings between Libya and Canada over Muammar Gaddafi's aborted trip to Canada in late September." The cable added: "Libya's moves against PetroCanada, set against the backdrop of an escalating conflict with Switzerland, have left the expatriate business community on edge. Libya's willingness to explicitly link commercial contracts to political disputes has only added to the international energy companies' growing frustration with the Libyan business climate."

Though it would be a stretch to say the regime opposed Western multinationals, some investors were unhappy about "Libyan resource nationalism", as a US State Department cable put it. In May 2012 the *Wall Street Journal* described how Western companies share of oil from each field steadily declined from 50 percent in 2004 to 12 percent before the conflict. The paper reported on foreign investors who "hoped regime change in Libya ... would bring relief in some of the tough terms they had agreed to in partnership deals" with the national oil company.

But, it was through this relatively nationalist oil policy that the 42-year dictator derived some legitimacy. By redistributing petrodollars Gaddafi could claim major socio-economic achievements, including high standards of healthcare and an 88 percent literacy rate. When Gaddafi took power in 1969 Libyan life expectancy was 51 years. It reached 74 years prior to the conflict. Libya also had the highest GDP per capita in Africa at $16,300 (as well as greater women's rights than many other Arab countries).

During the conflict the allied nations greatly increased their economic power over Libya. Militarily dependent on NATO for their victory, the NTC was also financially dependent on these same countries. Canada and other intervening countries controlled a great deal of Libya's international assets, which gave them leverage over the NTC's post-war economic policy. "Canadian companies will benefit from military intervention: Libyan official", explained a September Postmedia headline. Leading foreign policy journalist Lee Berthiaume wrote: "Libya's top diplomat in Ottawa expects Canadian companies to benefit from the goodwill earned by this country's active military involvement in the effort to topple Muammar Gaddafi's regime."

In the aftermath of Canada's intervention a slew of corporate lobbying organizations popped up, including the Free Libyan Chamber Of Commerce (Canada), Canada-Libya Trade Alliance and Canada-Libya Chamber of Commerce. On a January 2012 visit to Tripoli with representatives of 15 Canadian companies trade minister Fast attended the inauguration of the Libyan-Canadian Association of Co-operation and Development. "Since last September, we have had our trade commissioners on the ground in Libya," Fast boasted four months after Gaddafi's death. "And those trade commissioners are focused on re-establishing and expanding existing business connections and building new commercial relationships to support Libya's reconstruction in the year's ahead." The small team that reopened Canada's Tripoli embassy in September, a month before Gaddafi was killed, included a trade commissioner and an expert on commercial law. Four months later Postmedia noted that the embassy had no diplomats specializing in political or human rights issues.

When foreign minister Baird traveled to Libya just after Gaddafi's death a number of corporate executives accompanied him and when he met NTC officials in Paris in September a Suncor executive came along. In an end-of-2011 interview with *Diplomat and International Canada* minister Baird said: "We're there to promote our national interests, which is Canadian business and the economic prosperity of our country and Libya's."

War and profit have always marched together.

5. Best Friend of the Israeli Right

As the bombing of Libya illustrates sometimes foreign policy is determined by politics, in the sense that a political party uses an issue to promote itself. When the politics of an issue also aligns with powerful economic interests it is more likely that policy will be pursued. But sometimes neither narrow politics nor economic interests are sufficient to explain a government's foreign policy moves. Sometimes what one could describe as 'principle' — good or bad — helps determine policy towards another country or region of the world. Canada's relationship to Israel illustrates this aspect of foreign policy.

The Harper government has made Canada — at least diplomatically — the most pro-Israel country in the world. In February 2012, foreign minister Baird told an audience in Israel that "Israel has no greater friend in the world than Canada." During Baird's visit Israel's finance minister Yuval Steinitz joked: "I think Canada's an even better friend of Israel than we [Israelis] are." One commentator writing in *Israel Hayom* described Baird's comments this way: "When he discusses the Palestinian issue, Baird sounds like he could have voted in this week's [right-wing ruling party] Likud primaries."

As I argue in my book *Canada and Israel: Building Apartheid*, two of the most important sources of support for Israel are Christian Zionism and the view that Israel is a Western outpost in the Middle East. Harper's Conservative Party is home to both evangelical Christian Zionists and the most extreme proponents of Western rule over the rest of the world. In fact, one could argue that at the base of Harper's brand of neoconservatism is a coalition

of extreme pro-US capitalists and right-wing Christians. Uncritical support for Israel is a key 'principle' uniting this base. To keep these supporters happy the Conservatives take a 'principled stand' in support of a country much of the world sees as a serial breaker of international law.

Zionism is particularly strong among evangelicals who believe Jews need to "return" to the Middle East to hasten the second coming of Jesus and the Apocalypse. In April 2010 B'nai Brith's *Jewish Tribune* reported on a Conservative MP's speech to a major Christian Zionist event in Toronto. "Jeff Watson, Conservative MP for Essex, delivered greetings from Prime Minister Stephen Harper. The creation of the state of Israel fulfills God's promise in Deuteronomy to gather the Jewish people from all corners of the world, he said."

About 10 percent of Canadians identify as evangelicals (including the prime minister and a number of cabinet ministers). The president of the right-wing Canadian Centre for Policy Studies, Joseph Ben-Ami, explains: "The Jewish community in Canada is 380,000 strong; the evangelical community is 3.5 million. The real support base for Israel is Christians."

This country's leading Christian Zionist activist is Charles McVety. In charge of Canada Christian College and Christians United for Israel (Canada), McVety was close to many Conservative officials and apparently boasted (he disputes it) "I can pick up the phone and call Harper and I can get him in two minutes." In May 2011 McVety said: "Islam is not just a religion, it's a political and cultural system as well and we know that Christians, Jews and Hindus don't have the same mandate for a hostile takeover." McVety made this statement when Canada Christian College hosted Geert Wilders, a Dutch politician who

compared the Qur'an to Hitler's *Mein Kampf* and called for his country to ban the Muslim holy book. On Fox News Wilders said: "The border of jihad, the border between the West and the barbarism of the east, of Islam, and reason of the West is exactly the border between Israel and the Arab countries."

Christian Zionists often support an Islamophobic 'clash of civilizations' worldview and major swaths of the Conservative party consider Israel a Western outpost. "The existential threat faced by Israel on a daily basis is ultimately a threat to the broader Western civilization," said immigration minister Jason Kenney in May 2009. "It's a threat that comes from profoundly undemocratic forces that don't have the same conception of human dignity or freedom, and which abuse Israel as a kind of representative of the broader West and Western liberal-democratic values."

The geopolitical equation underlying this sentiment is rarely articulated explicitly in public but Canadian planners have long viewed Israel as a Western military outpost. In a 1952 memo to cabinet this country's most important post-World War II foreign policy decision-maker, Lester Pearson, wrote: "With the whole Arab world in a state of internal unrest and in the grip of mounting anti-western hysteria, Israel is beginning to emerge as the only stable element in the whole Middle East area." Pearson went on to explain how "Israel may assume an important role in Western defence as the southern pivot of current plans for the defence" of the Eastern Mediterranean. Conservative officials have said nearly as much in public. During a November 2011 press conference defence minister MacKay justified "deepening" military cooperation with Israel to counter "much more volatility ... throughout the Arab Spring and Summer and now Arab Fall and the cascading effects" the pro-democracy uprisings had on

the region. In other words, the fall of president Mubarak in Egypt weakened the US position in the Middle East, which made the West's relationship with Israel more important.

So, despite Israel's continued illegal settlement building in the West Bank and East Jerusalem, the Conservatives have repeatedly sided with Israel against world opinion and common sense. After discussing the matter with his Israeli counterpart Harper blocked consensus at the 2011 G8 summit on a reference to the internationally recognized 1967 borders as the basis for renewed Israeli-Palestinian negotiations. At the end of 2011 the Conservatives voted against a half dozen UN resolutions supporting Palestinian rights. In one instance 167 countries voted in favour while seven voted no (Canada, Israel, the US, Marshall Islands, Federated States of Micronesia, Nauru and Palau) and four abstained (Australia, Cameroon, Côte d'Ivoire and Tonga).

The Conservatives' diplomacy and public statements have received the lion's share of media attention but this represents a small part of the government's extreme pro-Israel position. Harper's government also worked to divide Palestinians, signed a border security agreement with Israel, expanded a free trade accord, tightened military ties, openly allowed Canadian charities to support illegal settlements and attacked those supporting the Palestinian cause in Canada. This extreme policy began as soon as the Conservatives entered government.

Two days after Harper won a minority government on January 23, 2006, Hamas won Canadian-monitored and facilitated legislative elections in Palestine. But quickly after assuming power Harper made Canada the first country (after Israel) to cut its assistance to the Palestinian Authority (PA). The aid cut-off, which was designed to sow division within Palestinian society, had

devastating social effects. "Open warfare among Gazan families a by-product of aid freeze," explained a *Globe and Mail* headline. In a bid to lessen division and avoid a full-fledged civil war, political factions representing more than 90 percent of the Palestinian Legislative Council established a unity government in March 2007. Still, the Conservatives shunned the new government. "It's our policy to have no contact with members of the government or deputy ministers," said Daniel Dugas, then foreign minister Peter MacKay's director of communications. When the Palestinian unity government's information minister traveled to Ottawa on a global peace tour MacKay refused to meet him. Mustafa Barghouti, who represented a secular party, told *Embassy*: "I think the Canadian government is the only government that is taking such a position, except for Israel. Even the United States has sent its consul general [in Jerusalem, Jacob Walles,] to meet with the Palestinian finance minister [Salam Fayyad]." Barghouti had already met the foreign ministers of Sweden and Norway, the Secretary-General of the UN and US Secretary of State Condoleezza Rice.

Why the intransigence? Harper wanted to sow division within Palestinian society by destroying the unity government. In fact, Washington and Ottawa pushed for war between Hamas and Fatah. A senior figure in the Israeli intelligence establishment explained: "Washington did not want a unity government. It wanted Fatah to wreck it and it sent [US Lieutenant-General Keith] Dayton to create and train a force that could overthrow Hamas. When Hamas pre-empts it, everyone cries foul, claiming it's a military putsch by Hamas — but who did the putsch?"

After Hamas officials were ousted from the PA in June 2007, the Conservatives restarted diplomatic relations and financial support. "The Government of Canada welcomes the

leadership of President Abbas and Prime Minister [Salam] Fayyad in establishing a government that Canada and the rest of the international community can work with," explained MacKay after the unity government's collapse. With Palestinian society divided and a more compliant authority in control of the West Bank, CIDA immediately contributed $8 million "in direct support to the new government." Then in December 2007 the Conservatives announced a five-year $300 million aid program to the Palestinians, which was largely designed to serve Israel's interests. A *Saint John Telegraph-Journal* headline explained: "Canada's aid to Palestine benefits Israel, foreign affairs minister says." In January 2008 foreign minister Maxime Bernier said: "We are doing that [providing aid to the PA] because we want Israel to be able to live in peace and security with its neighbours."

In the short term the primary aim of Canadian aid was to create a Palestinian security force "to ensure that the PA maintains control of the West Bank against Hamas," as Canadian Ambassador to Israel Jon Allen was quoted as saying by the *Canadian Jewish News*. American General Dayton, in charge of organizing a 10,000-member Palestinian security force, even admitted that he was strengthening Mahmoud Abbas' Fatah against Hamas, telling a US audience in May 2009 his force was "working against illegal Hamas activities." According to *Al Jazeera*, between 2007 and early 2011 PA security forces arrested some 10,000 suspected Hamas supporters.

The broader aim of the US-Canada-Britain initiated Palestinian security reform was to build a force to patrol Israel's occupied territories. Canadian Lieutenant-Colonel Ron Allison, "Dayton's chief of liaison in the West Bank" for a year, was quoted by his hometown newspaper saying: "The Dayton team was

concerned with enhancing security on the West Bank of Palestine and was all geared towards looking after and ensuring the security of Israel."

"We don't provide anything to the Palestinians," noted Dayton, "unless it has been thoroughly coordinated with the state of Israel and they agree to it." For instance, Israel's internal intelligence agency, the Shin-Bet, vets all of the Palestinian recruits. Brigadier-General Michael Herzog, chief of staff to defence minister Ehud Barak, explained the Israeli military's position: "We're very happy with what he's [Dayton] doing."

The Israelis supported Dayton's force as a way to keep the West Bank population under control. Like all colonial authorities throughout history Israel looked to compliant locals to take up the occupation's security burden. In a December 2011 article titled "[Ehud] Barak admires PA security forces for protecting [Israeli] settlers [in the West Bank]" a Palestinian news agency described an interview the Israeli defence minister gave to a Hebrew radio station. Writing in a July 2011 issue of the *London Review of Books* Adam Shatz explained: "The PA already uses the American-trained National Security Force to undermine efforts by Palestinians to challenge the occupation. (Hamas, in Gaza, has cracked down on protest even more harshly.) 'They are the police of the occupation,' Myassar Atyani, a leader of the Popular Front for the Liberation of Palestine, told me. 'Their leadership is not Palestinian, it is Israeli.' On 15 May – the day Palestinians commemorate their Nakba [the 1948 destruction of Palestinian society] – more than a thousand Palestinians, mainly young men, marched to the Qalandia checkpoint between Ramallah and Jerusalem and clashed with Israeli soldiers; but when Atyani tried to lead a group of demonstrators to the Hawara checkpoint outside

Nablus, PA security forces stopped them. The road from Ramallah to Qalandia is in Area C, which is not controlled by the PA; the road from Nablus to Hawara is in Area A, which is. And protesters who have attempted to march to settlements along PA-controlled roads have also found themselves turned back. It is an extraordinary arrangement: the security forces of a country under occupation are being subcontracted by third parties outside the region to prevent resistance to the occupying power, even as that power continues to grab more land. This is, not surprisingly, a source of considerable anger and shame in the West Bank."

Since the beginning of Dayton's mission numerous human rights reports noted deteriorating democratic rights in the West Bank. Many journalists and cartoonists were jailed and numerous online media outlets critical of Abbas were censored. Abbas' security force repeatedly suppressed peaceful demonstrations in Ramallah against the PA and Israel. For instance, "Dayton's men" (as Palestinians derisively dubbed them) disrupted demonstrations in the West Bank against Israel's brutal 22-day assault on Gaza in 2009. Similarly, they blocked pro Arab Spring protests in February 2011. In response, Human Rights Watch called on Western countries to suspend their aid to the Palestinian security forces.

The PA forces are widely believed to engage in torture. In the *Palestine Papers*, leaked diplomatic correspondence on Israel-Palestine peace negotiations, Dayton admitted "they are torturing people". A January 2011 *Foreign Policy* article titled "Building a police state in Palestine" notes that Western donors built 52 prisons — "more prisons than schools" — and at 1:80 the security force-to-population-ratio in the West Bank is among the highest in the world. In effect, Canada helped build a security apparatus to protect a corrupt PA led by Mahmoud Abbas, whose electoral mandate

expired in January 2009, but whom the Israeli government prefers over Hamas. The Conservative government invested heavily in PA security forces. Foreign minister MacKay met Dayton in Jerusalem two months before the Palestinian unity government collapsed and offered an immediate $1.2-million for his mission to destroy it. US secretary of state Condoleezza Rice said Dayton "has a Canadian counterpart with whom he works very closely." The new Palestinian security force was largely trained in Jordan at the US- built International Police Training Center (created to train Iraqi security after the 2003 invasion). In October 2009 the *Wall Street Journal* reported: "[Palestinian] recruits are trained in Jordan by Jordanian police, under the supervision of American, Canadian, and British officers." The number of military trainers in the West Bank varied slightly but in mid-2010, 18 Canadian troops worked with six British and ten US soldiers under Dayton's command. "The Canadian contribution is invaluable," explained Dayton. Canadians are particularly useful because "US personnel have travel restrictions when operating in the West Bank. But, our British and Canadian members do not." Calling them his "eyes and ears" Dayton said: "The Canadians ... are organized in teams we call road warriors, and they move around the West Bank daily visiting Palestinian security leaders, gauging local conditions."

Part of the US Security Coordinator office in Jerusalem, the Canadian military mission in the West Bank (dubbed Operation PROTEUS) included RCMP officers as well as officials from Foreign Affairs, Justice Canada and the Canadian Border Services Agency. In a September 2010 interview with the *Jerusalem Post* deputy foreign minister Peter Kent said Operation PROTEUS was Canada's "second largest deployment after Afghanistan" and it receives "most of the money" from the five-year $300 million

Canadian "aid" program to the Palestinians. During a February 2012 visit to Israel, foreign minister Baird told the *Globe and Mail* he was "incredibly thrilled" by the West Bank security situation, which he said benefited Israel. In regards to the training of Palestinian police, prosecutors and corrections officers the minister stated: "Canada considers this money well spent."

Canadian support for the PA security apparatus was supposed to be part of a "nation building" process. But there is little evidence that Israel is allowing a viable Palestinian state to be created. Growing Jewish settlements, Israeli bypass roads and the apartheid barrier all make a Palestinian state far from realistic in the short to medium term. And, when the usually compliant PA president, Mahmoud Abbas, made a (largely symbolic) bid for the UN to recognize Palestinian statehood in late 2011 the Conservatives opposed the effort. At the time Harper called it "very regrettable" while Baird labeled it a "public-relations" exercise, which in February 2012 he described as "profoundly wrong". Canada was one of only a half dozen countries that publicly criticized the PA's UN statehood bid and the Conservatives lobbied "like-minded" countries to do the same (despite the PA sending high-profile emissary Hanan Ashrawi to Ottawa to blunt such a move). On June 24, 2011, the *New York Times* reported: "Canada ... has been lobbying smaller countries to tell the Palestinians that they will not vote with them in September." Ten months later the *Globe and Mail* reported on internal documents showing that foreign minister Baird called at least eight of his counterparts in other countries to persuade them against voting with the Palestinians. In an effort to spare the US and Israel from complete isolation the Conservatives spent this country's diminishing diplomatic currency trying to cobble together a group of countries to vote against Palestinian statehood.

Despite Canadian-Israeli-American efforts, the Palestinians received widespread international backing. Voting 107 to 14 (with 52 abstentions) the United Nations Educational, Scientific and Cultural Organization (UNESCO) was the first arm of the international body to grant Palestine full membership rights. In protest Baird threatened to withdraw Canadian funding from the organization (as the US did). "We are not happy with the decision UNESCO has made, and we have to look and see what we should do in response," he said. Canada eventually decided to continue payments already committed but all new requests from the organization would be denied. "Under no circumstances will Canada be contributing more money to cover any budgetary shortfall that may result from this decision. Those countries that voted in favour of the Palestinian proposal ought to have known the potential financial implications this would have."

Opposed to Abbas' statehood bid, Harper backed Israel's onslaught against the 1.6 million Palestinians in Gaza. For dozens of months Israel reduced food and medicine from entering the tiny coastal territory to a fraction of what was needed, but the Harper government refused to criticize the siege. For example, Canada was the only country at the UN Human Rights Council to vote against a January 2008 resolution that called for "urgent international action to put an immediate end to the siege of the occupied Gaza Strip". The motion was adopted with 30 votes in favour and 15 abstentions.

After killing 120 in March 2008, Israel unleashed a 22-day military assault on Gaza at the end of 2008 that left 1,400, mostly civilians, dead. Ottawa wholeheartedly supported this campaign. "Canada's position has been well known from the very beginning. Hamas is a terrorist group. Israel defended itself,"

foreign minister Cannon proclaimed, even though only 13 Israelis (three of whom were civilians) died during the 22-day assault. Ottawa even justified Israel's killing of 40 Palestinian civilians at a UN–run school. Deputy foreign minister Kent said: "We really don't have complete details yet, other than the fact that we know that Hamas has made a habit of using civilians and civilian infrastructure as shields for their terrorist activities, and that would seem to be the case again today." Kent added that Hamas "bears the full responsibility for the deepening humanitarian tragedy. ... In many ways, Hamas behaves as if they are trying to have more of their people killed to make a terrible terrorist point." Presumably the "terrible terrorist point" was that the Israeli army brutally murders Palestinian civilians. It's not hard to prove.

Compared to Ottawa's cheerleading, most of the world was hostile to Israel's actions. Many countries criticized the killing of civilians. In solidarity with Gaza, Venezuela expelled Israel's ambassador at the start of the bombardment and broke off all diplomatic relations two weeks later. Israel didn't need to worry, since Ottawa was prepared to help out. The Canadian embassy in Caracas took over Israel's diplomatic relations there. Canada officially became Israel, at least in Venezuela.

While many governments criticized Israel's actions in Gaza international solidarity activists decided to directly challenge the siege. On May 31, 2010, Israeli commandos raided a flotilla of ships carrying 10,000 tonnes of humanitarian supplies and more than 600 activists to Gaza. Nine civilians were killed and dozens more wounded in this attack in international waters. Governments around the world strongly condemned Israel's actions. Turkey's Prime Minister Recep Tayyip Erdogan called the raid "an act of inhumane state terrorism".

The Canadian government took a much different approach. Only 10 hours after the raid, Harper held pre-scheduled talks with Israeli Prime Minister Benjamin Netanyahu in Ottawa and his office simply said it "deeply regrets" the loss of life and injuries.

When another flotilla, including a Canadian-flagged ship, prepared to breach the siege a year later, Foreign Affairs issued a "statement with the hope of dissuading Canadians from participating in similar flotillas." In the statement minister Baird proclaimed the flotilla "unauthorized" and "provocative". He said: "Canada recognizes Israel's legitimate security concerns and its right to protect itself and its residents from attacks by Hamas and other terrorist groups, including by preventing the smuggling of weapons."

In November 2011 the Canadian Boat to Gaza eventually set sail from Turkey. The Israeli navy captured the Canadian-flagged boat in international waters, a violation of international law, with no protest from Ottawa. Instead, Foreign Affairs criticized the political-humanitarian mission and the Canadians imprisoned, tasered and robbed by the Israelis.

Beyond defending Israel's position, the Harper government directly participated in Israel's siege of Gaza. In early 2009, Canada joined the Gaza Counter-Arms Smuggling Initiative alongside the Netherlands, France, Germany, Norway, Denmark, Italy and the US (Israel was an observer at meetings). "We look forward to continuing work with our partners on the program of action to coordinate efforts to stop the flow of arms, ammunition and related material into the Gaza Strip," foreign minister Cannon said in a June 2009 statement. He, of course, was not referring to Israel Defense Forces weaponry, which killed thousands in Gaza.

The Gaza Counter-Arms Smuggling Initiative, which meets regularly, is an intelligence/military network designed to strengthen Israel's position in the region. In a November 2011 speech titled "Ensuring Israel's Qualitative Military Edge" US assistant secretary of political-military affairs, Andrew J. Shapiro, described the Counter-Arms Smuggling Initiative as "a broad range of diplomatic, military, intelligence and law enforcement tools to stop the shipment of arms, especially rockets and missiles into Gaza that threaten neighbouring Israeli communities."

Impressed by Israel's covert war on Iran, bombing of Lebanon and subjugation of Palestinians, the Conservatives greatly expanded intelligence/military cooperation. In early 2008 Ottawa signed a wide-ranging "border management and security" agreement with Israel, even though the two countries do not share a border. The agreement is rather vague, but includes sharing information as well as cooperating on illegal immigration and law enforcement. This accord is likely an attempt to formalize some aspects of the Canadian Security and Intelligence Service's relationship with Mossad, Israel's international intelligence agency.

Since the election of the first Harper government Canada-Israel military ties have also grown. According to a June 2012 CBC summary of government briefing notes, "the [two] countries have agreed to exchange secret defence information." Both countries' top generals and defence ministers visited each other's country in a bid to forge tighter military bonds. In March 2012 Israel's military chief, Benny Gantz, visited Canada "to build upon the Principal Memorandum of Understanding (PMOU) signed by Canada and Israel in January 2011, and to strengthen existing ties by underlining the practical benefits of our growing defence

relationship." For the first time in its history, in 2011, Israel named a defence attaché, Brigadier General Eden Attias to Ottawa.

Until at least the end of 2010 the Canadian embassy in Tel Aviv served as Israel's Contact Point Embassy to NATO, the military alliance of Western nations. The embassy served as the liaison between Israel and NATO, assisting with visits of NATO officials to Israel. According to internal government documents examined by *The Dominion*, Ottawa worked to strengthen Israel's partnership with the military alliance, helping its "pursuit of a Status of Forces Agreement, getting access to the NATO Maintenance Supply Agency, [redacted]." In February 2010 deputy foreign minister Kent implied that Canada already considered Israel a member of NATO, which operates according to the principle that an attack on any member is considered an attack against all members. Reflecting the alliance's purported principle, Kent said "an attack on Israel would be considered an attack on Canada" and in July 2011 defence minister MacKay reiterated this position privately. According to briefing notes uncovered by CBC he told Israel's top military commander, Gabi Ashkenazi, that "a threat to Israel is a threat to Canada."

Relations between the two countries' military industries grew as well. At a November 2011 press conference with his Israeli counterpart defence minister MacKay described the two countries' "growing relations in the defence sector." The Canadian military bought the Israeli-made Heron drone for use in Afghanistan and Israel's Elisra Electronics Systems worked on upgrading a dozen Halifax-class warships. Despite the IDF's many human rights violations, Canadian companies sold weapons directly to Israel. According to an early 2009 Coalition to Oppose the Arms Trade report, more than 140 Canadian weapons makers export products

to Israel. The December 2011 *Washington Report on Middle East Affairs* detailed some Canadian military exports to Israel. "Ottawa's Allen Vanguard Corporation provides 'counterterrorist' equipment and training. iMPath Networks of Ottawa and Halifax design solutions for real-time video surveillance and intrusion detection technology. Mecachrome Technologies, based in Montréal and Toronto, provides components for military aircraft. And MPB Technologies of Pointe Claire, Edmonton, Airdrie and Calgary manufacturers, among other things, communications equipment and robotics for [Israeli] military use. ... British Columbia-based 360 Surveillance sells technology for Israel's apartheid wall and checkpoints." In June 2012 BC-based MacDonald, Dettwiler and Associates won a \$90+ million contract to supply Israel Aerospace Industries with satellite technology.

Taxpayers often underwrite ties between Canadian and Israeli military companies. In July 2011 the Conservatives allocated another \$5-million to the Canada-Israel Industrial Research and Development Foundation, which funds research projects (including many in the "security" field) between the two countries' corporations.

The 1997 Canada-Israel Free Trade Agreement also facilitates cross-country corporate ties. In October 2010, the Conservatives announced that Canada and Israel would be "modernizing" this "first-generation" trade agreement "by significantly expanding its application." In an implicit recognition of the occupation, Canada's free trade accord with Israel includes the West Bank as a place where the country's custom laws apply. Canada's trade agreement is based on the areas Israel maintains territorial control over, not on internationally recognized borders. The European Union's trade agreement with Israel, on the other

hand, explicitly excludes products from territory Israel captured in the 1967 war and occupies against international law.

A topic ignored by the dominant media, the Conservatives have embraced tax write-offs for illegal Israeli settlements. Guelph activist Dan Maitland emailed foreign minister Cannon concerning Canada Park, a Jewish National Fund of Canada initiative built on land Israel occupied after the June 1967 War (three Palestinian villages were demolished to make way for the park). In August 2010 Maitland received a reply from Keith Ashfield, national revenue minister, who refused to discuss the particulars of the case but provided "general information about registered charities and the occupied territories." Ashfield wrote "the fact that charitable activities take place in the occupied territories is not a barrier to acquiring or maintaining charitable status." This means Canadian organizations can openly fundraise for settlements illegal under international law and get the government to pay up to a third of the cost through tax credits for donations. To justify the government's position, Ashfield cited a September 2002 Federal Court of Appeal case (Canadian Magen David Adom for Israel v. Minister of National Revenue), which reversed the Canada Revenue Agency's previous position.

The exact amount is not known but it's safe to assume that millions of Canadian dollars make their way to Israeli settlements annually. Every year Canadians send a few hundred million dollars in tax-deductible donations to Israeli universities, parks, immigration initiatives and, more controversially, "charities" that aid the Israeli army in one way or another.

While a number of Jewish groups publicly promote their support for the IDF few Jewish charities openly tout their support for those stealing Palestinian land in violation of international

law. Interestingly, it appears that Christian Zionist groups are more explicit about their support for West Bank settlers. One such charity registered with Ottawa, Christian Friends of Israeli Communities (CFOIC), says it supports "the Jews currently living in Biblical Israel – the communities of Judea and Samaria (and previously Gaza)." Judea and Samaria is the biblical term right wing Israelis use to describe the occupied West Bank. CFOIC explain that they "provide Christians with deeper insight into the significance of Judea and Samaria — the heartland of Israel — and the people who live there. This is done by bringing groups of Christians to visit the communities, and providing information about the communities on an ongoing basis; and provide financial and moral support to the Jewish communities who are developing the land in faithfulness to their God."

While it is legal — and government will foot part of the bill — to finance charities linked to settlements that contravene international law, it's illegal for Canadians to aid a hospital overseen by the elected Hamas government in Gaza. The Conservatives reinforced Canada's post 9-11 terrorist list that makes it illegal to financially assist groups associated with these organizations. In December 2010 Hamas criticized the Conservatives for re-listing it a "terrorist" entity. "The decision is a clear bias to Israel," Hamas spokesman Fawzi Barhoum told Chinese news agency Xinhua. "This encourages Israel to commit more crimes against the Palestinian people."

A provision in the Harper government's 2012 omnibus crime bill, the Justice for Victims of Terrorism Act, may further deter individuals from donating to Palestinian charities. Nicholas Pengelley, a law professor at Queen's University, explains: "The Act provides that a person may bring an action to recover damages

for any act that would be punishable in Canada under sections 83.02 to 83.04 and 83.18 to 83.23 of the Criminal Code. One such section (Section 83.03) provides: 'Every one who, directly or indirectly, collects property, provides or invites a person to provide, or makes available property or financial or other related services ... is guilty of an indictable offence and is liable to imprisonment for a term of not more than 10 years.' With this in mind, suppose that a Canadian visitor to Israel is killed or injured in a bomb blast blamed on Hamas. Further suppose that a Canadian citizen or organization has donated to a charity to support purchase of, say, a kidney machine to be supplied to a hospital in Gaza. In order to get that kidney machine installed in the Gaza hospital, negotiations have taken place with the Hamas-controlled Ministry of Health. Perhaps the funds were even funnelled through that ministry as the most efficient way to achieve the desired goal.

"The Canadian government lists Hamas as a terrorist organization. Once the Act becomes law, and its ramifications become known, it cannot be doubted that the 'fear factor' ... will considerably diminish the pool of donors willing to risk lawsuits, not to mention the possibility of imprisonment."

Pengelley's hypothetical scenario was based on a case brought against the International Relief Fund for the Afflicted and Needy (IRFAN), which was accused of ties to Hamas. This case illustrates the flagrant double standard between how the government treats charities working in Israel versus those helping the much poorer Palestinians. A Toronto-based Muslim charity, IRFAN raised a few million dollars annually for projects in a dozen countries. At its high point the group sponsored four thousand orphans. In November 2004 then opposition MP Stockwell Day, backed by the pro-Israel Canadian Coalition for Democracies,

called on the Liberal government to investigate IRFAN for any ties to Hamas. The Canada Revenue Agency (CRA) investigated the group but failed to register a serious complaint. Soon after the Conservatives took office, the CRA audited IRFAN again. In April 2011 the CRA revoked the group's charitable status, claiming "IRFAN-Canada is an integral part of an international fundraising effort to support Hamas." A big part of the CRA's supporting evidence was that IRFAN worked with the Gaza Ministry of Health and Ministry of Telecommunications, which came under Hamas' direction after they won the 2006 election. The Toronto-based organization tried to send a dialysis machine to Gaza and continued to support orphans in the impoverished territory with the money channeled through the Post Office controlled by the Telecommunications Ministry.

This author cannot claim any detailed knowledge of the charity, but on the surface of it the charge that IRFAN was a front for Hamas makes little sense. First of all, the group was registered with the Palestinian Authority in the West Bank when the Fatah-controlled PA was waging war against Hamas. Are we to believe that CRA officials in Ottawa had a better sense of who supported Hamas then the PA in Ramallah? Additionally, the United Nations Relief and Works Agency (UNRWA) viewed the Canadian charity as a legitimate partner. In 2009 IRFAN gave UNRWA $1.2 million to build a school for girls in Battir, a West Bank village.

The CRA spent hundreds of thousands of dollars investigating IRFAN. It appears that the Revenue Agency wanted to help their Conservative bosses prove that Muslim Canadians financed "Hamas terror".

In putting together an elaborate response to the CRA's accusations, the charity wanted to dissuade pro-Israel groups

from pursuing criminal charges. Since none of the charity's board members were charged with aiding terrorists after the CRA withdrew IRFAN's charitable status this appears to have been successful. Nevertheless, that threat remains real.

Just like IRFAN, groups in any way associated with the Palestinian cause were openly attacked. In early 2009 government funding for the Canadian Arab Federation's language instruction to new immigrants was cut after the organization criticized the Conservatives' unflinching support for Israel's onslaught against the Palestinians. Similarly, government support for Palestine House's immigration program was eliminated at the start of 2012. The government chopped $7 million from Kairos, a Christian aid organization that had received government money for 35 years. During a December 2009 visit to Israel immigration minister Jason Kenney said Canada "defunded organizations, most recently like Kairos, who are taking a leadership role" in campaigns to boycott Israel (while sympathetic to Palestinians Kairos Canada, unlike the unaffiliated Kairos Palestine, did not endorse the boycott campaign).

The Conservatives chose a different tactic with the arm's-length government agency, Rights and Democracy. Instead of cutting its budget, they stacked the board with hard-line supporters of Israel. In February 2010 *Maclean's* reported: "The Rights and Democracy board is now predominantly composed of people who have devoted much of their life to an unequivocal position: that no legal challenge to Israel's human rights record is permissible, because any such challenge is part of a global harassment campaign against Israel's right to exist."

The new 'Israel no matter what' board members hounded the organization's president, Remy Beauregard, until he died of a heart attack after a "vitriolic" meeting. Once in charge, the new

board voted to "repudiate" three $10,000 grants given to Israeli and Palestinian human rights groups (B'Tselem, Al-Haq and Al-Mezan). And, the *Toronto Star* reported, the "Conservative-appointed [R&D] board secretly decided to close the agency's Geneva office, distancing itself from a United Nations body it viewed as anti-Israeli."

Some of those supporting the Palestinian cause at the grassroots level faced a different threat. There is evidence that CSIS tried to intimidate and spy on pro-Palestinian Canadians. Twice in one week in August 2010 CSIS agents visited the home of Ehab Lotayef, one of the Canadian Boat to Gaza organizers. The agents claimed to be concerned that unfriendly individuals might take advantage of the endeavour, but this followed their harassment of other pro-Palestinian activists.

On April 7, 2010, Freda Guttman, a 76-year-old Jewish Montréaler, received a visit from CSIS agents. She slammed the door on them so it's not clear if the visit was related to her role in Tadamon!, a Middle East solidarity collective, or her friendship with Canadian activist Stefan Christoff. A tall, mild-mannered 30-year-old, Christoff was one of Montréal's most effective grassroots activists. Involved with various issues, he worked on Palestinian solidarity with Tadamon! and the highly successful Artists Against Apartheid (AAA) campaign. Beginning in 2007 AAA organized more than a dozen concerts and brought together 500 Québec artists in support of the Boycott Divestment and Sanctions campaign, which supporters of Israel view as a major threat. At the start of 2010 CSIS agents visited seven of Christoff's friends. These unannounced visits usually took place early in the morning. The agents asked questions about Christoff's trips to the Middle East or Artists Against Apartheid and in some instances,

they feigned concern for the Palestinian cause, implying Christoff's radical activist roots might hurt it.

As a national intelligence organization shrouded in secrecy, it is hard to know if CSIS was mandated to target Palestine solidarity activists. But, considering Harper's attitude it's not surprising that CSIS officials view anyone defending Palestinian rights as a threat.

The Conservatives repeatedly equated expressions of support for Palestinian rights with extremism. In March 2009, Ottawa barred British parliamentarian George Galloway from Canada for delivering humanitarian aid to Hamas officials who were the elected administration in Gaza. At the start of 2010 the Conservatives attempted to pass a condemnation of Israeli Apartheid Week in Parliament ("this House is concerned about expressions of anti-Semitism under the guise of 'Israeli Apartheid Week'"). In mid-2010 Harper accused Libby Davies, deputy leader of the NDP, of making "extremist" statements because she gave halting support to the boycott/divestment/sanctions (BDS) campaign and said Israel had been occupying Palestinian territories since 1948. Demanding Davies be fired as the NDP's deputy leader, Harper told the House of Commons "she made statements that could have been made by Hamas, Hezbollah," which Canada considers terrorist organizations.

The Conservatives also worked to delegitimize the pro-Palestinian movement in other ways. They repeatedly equated criticism of Israel with racism towards Jews. "I guess my fear is what I see happening in some circles is anti-Israeli sentiment, really just as a thinly disguised veil for good old-fashioned anti-Semitism," Harper said in a May 2008 interview with Montreal's CJAD radio. "We learned in the Second World War that those

who would hate and destroy the Jewish people would ultimately hate and destroy the rest of us as well, and the same holds today." Two and a half years later he denounced the "new anti-Semitism" before the Inter-Parliamentary Coalition for Combating Anti-Semitism in Ottawa. "Harnessing disparate anti-American, anti-Semitic and anti-Western ideologies, it targets the Jewish people by targeting the Jewish homeland, Israel, as the source of injustice and conflict in the world and uses, perversely, the language of human rights to do so." In May 2012 Baird declared: "We contend that modern anti-Semitism lives in the disproportionate criticism Israel receives, and the refusal to accept its right to exist... The world cannot take the words of Hamas, Hezbollah and Iran as mere rhetoric and risk appeasing these malicious actors in the same way the world appeased the Nazis."

The Conservatives are so single-mindedly pro-Israel that any criticism of that state must be denounced in the harshest terms possible. Their "principled" position amounts to this: Israel can do no wrong.

6. At War with Lebanon and Iran

The foreign policy that flows from being Israel's best friend and one of the main cheerleaders of the neoconservative world order is more militaristic than what most Canadians are comfortable with. This has included extreme belligerence and support for other countries' wars, which is clearly seen in their positions on the invasion of Lebanon and the threatened attack against Iran.

Lebanon

Because of his "principles" Harper defended Israel's summer 2006 invasion, Israel's fifth, of Lebanon. When he told reporters that Israel's military assault on Lebanon was a "measured response" to Hezbollah incursions, Harper probably regretted it. Two days later, Israel wiped out an entire Lebanese-Canadian family, including four children aged one to eight. Harper's comment brought the kind of publicity even a staunchly pro-Israel prime minister could not like. But, with 1,100 (mostly civilian) Lebanese dead and much of the country's infrastructure destroyed, the Conservatives continued to endorse Israel's aggression. Three months after the conclusion of hostilities, Harper vetoed a 55-member Francophonie statement that "'deplored' the effect of the month-long conflict on the Lebanese civilians it endangered." For Harper the statement was too one-sided, even if the 33-day war caused more than ten times the deaths on the Lebanese side, in a country with a little more than half of Israel's population. In December 2011 the UN General Assembly again called on Israel to compensate Lebanon for the damages caused during the 2006

war. One hundred and sixty five countries voted in favour of the resolution. Eight, including Canada, voted against while six abstained and 14 nations were absent.

During its bombing of Lebanon Israel destroyed a UN compound, killing Canadian Major Paeta Hess-Von Kruedener. At the time of the bombing Harper publicly questioned the UN for keeping its forces in the war zone and demanded answers. When a UN inquiry concluded that on the day of the fatal bombing, Hezbollah fighters were nowhere near the UN post the "pro military" Conservative government ignored the report. In fact, internal documents uncovered by *The Dominion* refer to a letter Harper wrote Israeli Prime Minister Ehud Olmert soon after the incident accepting that country's account of the incident.

After the war protests erupted against the Lebanese government's close ties to the US and Saudi Arabia and general indifference to the Israeli assault. Lebanon was split into two broad political camps: the Saudi/Western backed March 14 coalition and the Iran/Syria supported March 8 group. The Conservatives strengthened their relations with the Lebanese groups least resistant to Israel's aggression. Canada followed Washington's lead in arming the Lebanese army as a counterweight to Hezbollah's military force, reported the *New York Times* in October 2008.

Ottawa repeatedly declared its support for the pro-Western anti-Hezbollah faction during the political crisis that followed the war. In November 2006 Foreign Affairs noted: "Canada stands firmly by Prime Minister Fouad Siniora and his government in these challenging times." Another release seven months later explained: "Canada applauds the leadership of Prime Minister Fouad Siniora at this critical juncture in Lebanon's history." Two years later they declared: "We also congratulate

Sa'ad Hariri and the members of the 14 March coalition on their [election] victory."

The Conservatives took a different tack with Hezbollah ("Lebanon's largest political party and most potent armed force" in the words of the *Los Angeles Times*) and the leading member of the March 8 coalition. The month after Hezbollah successfully held off the Israeli invasion foreign minister MacKay said: "Lebanon is being held hostage by Hezbollah. There can be no doubt about that. Hezbollah is a cancer on Lebanon, which is destroying stability and democracy within its boundaries."

A couple months later MacKay called Hezbollah the "Taliban on steroids." For his part, public safety minister Stockwell Day claimed the "stated intent of Hezbollah is to annihilate Jewish people." Jason Kenney echoed this statement in September 2009, saying Hezbollah is "motivated by a profound anti-Semitism." (Despite Kenney and Day's claims, Hezbollah was created in response to Israel's 1982-2000 occupation of southern Lebanon and its pronouncements suggest it is largely concerned with Israel's occupation of Arab lands.) The Conservatives' demonization of Hezbollah gathered steam when Daniel Bellemare, a Canadian official, took charge of the international investigation into the February 2005 assassination of five-time Lebanese premier Rafik Hariri. In November 2007 Bellemare, deputy attorney general and special advisor to the deputy minister of justice until October 2007, was appointed commissioner of the United Nations International Independent Investigation Commission (UNIIIC) into the bombing that killed Hariri and two dozen others. Concurrently, he was named prosecutor of the Special Tribunal for Lebanon (STL), which was set to continue the UNIIIC's work beginning in March 2009.

Both the internal and international investigations into Hariri's killing were far from conclusive. Initially, Syrian security officers were implicated in the killings and in the post-assassination upheaval Syrian troops were driven from the country. Four Lebanese generals were also incarcerated for four years in the killings but they were released when the evidence against them was dismissed. In 2010 the STL began to point its finger at Hezbollah and in August 2011 four members of the Party of God were formally charged in the Hariri killings. But before the charges came down the international investigation was discredited in the eyes of many. A July 2011 survey of 800 Lebanese, sponsored by leading Arabic-language daily *As-Safir,* found that 60 percent of the country believed the international probe was politicized. The poll also found widespread distrust of Bellemare, who was accused of being pro-Israel and anti-Hezbollah. He also had suspiciously close relations with US officials.

Just after Bellemare issued the indictments against four individuals with ties to Hezbollah Lebanese daily *Al Akbar* published a detailed article on the Canadian titled "UN Tribunal: A Prosecutor's 'Tunnel Vision'" (translated by its English edition). "An example of this bias appears in paragraph 59 of the indictment, where Bellemare states that 'all four accused are supporters of Hezbollah, which is a political and military organization in Lebanon. In the past, the military wing of Hezbollah has been implicated in terrorist acts.' Bellemare does not offer a reference supporting his assertion that Hezbollah was involved in terrorism, and, so far, no international judicial body has issued a decision describing Hezbollah as a terrorist organization. In fact, there is no international consensus surrounding Hezbollah's 'terrorism' status, and the UN does not recognize Hezbollah as a terrorist organization.

Several countries, including the US, Israel, and Canada have officially labelled the group as a terrorist organization — though, notably, the European Union has not. Bellemare seemingly chose to include his personal political opinion and perhaps the views of some of his colleagues in an international indictment."

Many Lebanese believe the Israeli intelligence agency Mossad had a hand in Hariri's death yet Bellemare refused to say if he interviewed any Israeli suspects. A TV station linked to Hezbollah, *Al Manar*, claimed Bellemare "lost credibility" for his "politicized tribunal" because he was unwilling to investigate Israel's possible implication in the killings. The "Israeli enemy is 'innocent' and will remain so in the eyes of the international community and the STL Prosecutor Daniel Bellemare." The most damning evidence against Bellemare came from the US State Department. A series of US diplomatic cables, released by Wikileaks, suggest he worked closely with the US embassy in Beirut. On one occasion Bellemare asked US officials for information on Syria and for help in convincing the British to assist an investigation committee. The former deputy attorney general also requested two temporary FBI investigators be paid by the US. An October 2008 cable from the ambassador in Beirut to Washington read: "Bellemare showed a good understanding of the problems [for the US] associated with complying ... but his frustration was nonetheless evident: 'You are the key player [he said]. If the US doesn't help me, who will?'" The US embassy gave Bellemare "an 'excellence' preliminary assessment for his effort and determination, and we urge Washington to exert every effort to respond to the investigation committee's request related to the information and support." Hezbollah claimed the Wikileaks cables confirmed that the US manipulated the probe. "The

information leaked on meetings between the prosecutor and the US ambassador confirms what we have always said — that the US administration is using the court and the investigation committee as a tool to target the resistance [to Israel, i.e. Hezbollah]," noted Hezbollah MP Hassan Fadlallah in December 2010.

In January 2011 the Lebanese government collapsed when 10 cabinet ministers and one presidential appointee withdrew over then Prime Minister Saad Hariri's refusal to reject the STL. At the start of 2011 many feared that the STL's expected indictment of Hezbollah members could re-ignite the country's civil war, which lasted from 1975-1990. This didn't bother Washington. Secretary of State Hillary Clinton spoke in favour of the STL and announced $10 million in added funding for the floundering Tribunal. The US ambassador in Lebanon Maura Connelly said "the Special Tribunal for Lebanon (STL) is an irrevocable, international judicial process; its work is not a matter of politics but of law." Even President Obama chimed in, saying the STL's first indictment could end an "era of impunity" and that it was "a significant and emotional time for the Lebanese people."

In the first 10 weeks of 2011 Foreign Affairs released three statements that dealt with the STL. On January 13 the ministry complained about the dissolution of Lebanon's government over the matter. "These resignations are an attempt to subvert a safe and secure Lebanon and cannot be tolerated. Hezbollah's actions in bringing down the government are a clear attempt to undermine the Special Tribunal for Lebanon. Canada believes that the work of the Special Tribunal should go forward so that justice can be served." A follow-up statement explained: "We urge the future Lebanese government to continue to support and cooperate with the Tribunal and to continue to uphold its obligations under UN

Security Council resolutions on Lebanon." In March 2011 the Conservatives gave a further $1 million contribution to the STL. "Canada has been a strong supporter of the Tribunal, having already contributed $3.7 million to the voluntarily funded Tribunal since 2007," explained foreign minister Cannon.

An August 2011 Canadian Security Intelligence Service (CSIS) report, detailed in Montréal daily *La Presse*, found that "many Lebanese consider the work of the STL an inquest led by Canadians." At the time more than 20 Canadians were involved in the Tribunal's work and in February 2012 another Canadian replaced Bellemare. According to CSIS, this country's association with the highly divisive tribunal increased the likelihood of Canadians being targeted.

In Lebanon, as elsewhere, the Conservatives chose a side, which just happened to be the same side as elite interests in the US and Israel. But one is left to wonder if this is the foreign policy ordinary Canadians would choose if they were left to decide.

Iran

Another place the Conservatives took a side to impress their friends is Iran, where Canada has few major interests. But that country does have huge oil reserves, which has meant that over the last century it has been a constant target of superpower conquest, in one form or another. In the twentieth century first the British and then the US dominated the country's political system and economy.

Ever since the Shah was overthrown in 1979, and along with it American control, the US and its allies have tried to undermine Iran's leadership. In recent years the US and Israel have waged a low-level war against the country. Some Iranian

scientists have been assassinated, the country's computer structure sabotaged and its economy attacked. At the same time the US distributed hundreds of millions of dollars to violent and non-violent opposition groups.

Harper has enthusiastically backed the US/Israeli campaign against Iran. Conservative officials compared Iranian president Mahmoud Ahmadinejad to Hitler and the prime minister claimed Iran's leaders "frighten me". In January 2012 Harper told a Calgary radio station "Iran… is the world's most serious threat to international peace and security."

Despite both US and Israeli intelligence agencies concluding that there was no proof of an Iranian nuclear arms program, the prime minister told the CBC's Peter Mansbridge in February 2012 it was "beyond any doubt" Iran was working to develop nuclear weapons. Harper went on to say he was "absolutely convinced" Iran "would have no hesitation about using nuclear weapons."

As Canadian Peace Alliance co-chair Derrick O'Keefe pointed out: "This last comment is extraordinary; Harper is in effect claiming to know for a fact that the regime in Tehran is suicidal … Any attack by Iran, let alone its use of hypothetical nuclear weapons, would result in its total obliteration."

Harper used his pulpit as host of the 2010 G8/G20 to attack Iran. "Canada will use its G8 presidency to continue to focus international attention and action on the Iranian regime," explained the prime minister. During the lead up to the G20 meetings Ottawa criticized China, a key trading partner of Iran, for refusing to follow Western dictates regarding the Islamic Republic. "I think China should step up to the plate and do something here," foreign minister Cannon said.

Four years earlier, the *National Post* reported that Iran's parliament passed a Nazi-like law requiring Jews to wear coloured labels in public. Harper excitedly jumped on the May 2006 front-page report. "Unfortunately, we've seen enough already from the Iranian regime to suggest that it is very capable of this kind of action," the prime minister declared. Ignoring the fact Jews are represented in Iran's parliament, Harper claimed: "We've seen a number of things from the Iranian regime that are along these lines … It boggles the mind that any regime on the face of the Earth would want to do anything that could remind people of Nazi Germany." Of course, the story was completely false.

Even though Iran is more democratic and less repressive than a number of its neighbours, the Conservatives have incessantly attacked Iran's human rights record. They sponsored an annual UN resolution condemning Iran's "ongoing systematic violations of human rights." In November 2007, Steven Edwards, CanWest's reporter at the UN, wrote: "In what one western diplomat described as a 'division of labour', among western governments to keep up the pressure on Iran, the big European powers and the United States lead western efforts to convince Iran to roll back its nuclear program while Canada has spearheaded resolutions denouncing the way Iran treats huge numbers of its people."

Although uninterested in the oppression faced by Shia Muslims in Saudi Arabia or Bahrain, the Conservatives have devoted significant attention to Iran's oppressed religious minorities. A September 2, 2011, Foreign Affairs statement explained: "Canada calls on Iran to release individuals who have been arrested on the basis of their faith." Six weeks later minister Baird said: "Canada remains deeply concerned by the ongoing persecution of religious minorities in Iran, including members

of the Baha'i and Christian communities." Some speculated that Foreign Affairs set up its Office of Religious Freedom in 2012 partly to draw attention to the persecution of Christians, Baha'i and other religious minorities in Iran.

In an interesting twist, the Iranians responded with a campaign to undercut the Conservatives moral authority by drawing attention to Canada's human rights abuses. Largely unreported in this country, Iran's English language media published a slew of government statements criticizing Canada's human rights record. One December 2011 *Press TV* article noted: "[Iran's Foreign Ministry spokesman Ramin] Mehmanparast denounced the Canadian government's conduct towards Canada's aboriginal population in the Attawapiskat region of northern Ontario province and called on the United Nations to probe human rights violations in the area." Another from the *Tehran Times* in September 2011 explained: "The Iranian Foreign Ministry issued a statement on Thursday condemning the inhuman conditions that the indigenous people of Canada are experiencing." Still another noted: "The Iranian Foreign Ministry has expressed concerns over the treatment of protesters at the recent G20 summit in Toronto, Canada."

Attacking the regime's human rights record was only part of the Conservatives' campaign against Iran. Ottawa tried to squeeze that country on all fronts. They all but severed diplomatic relations with Iran and the Conservatives pursued sanctions in line with those of the US and Britain. Canadian sanctions against Iran blocked virtually all transactions, including with the country's central bank. The severity of the sanctions was driven home in the summer of 2012 when Toronto Dominion began canceling the bank accounts of Iranian Canadians who had received money from, or transferred money to, Iran.

146

Canada has also contributed to the war on Iran in other ways. For example, Ottawa was accused of spying for the US. In late 2006 members of the Iranian parliament claimed the Canadian embassy in Tehran was a "den of spies." In addition, for many years Canadian soldiers occupied Afghanistan, a country bordering Iran. This has not ended. In February 2012 the Canadian Press reported that small numbers of Canadian military trainers were sent to Herat in western Afghanistan, near the border with Iran.

For much of Harper's time in office the Canadian navy patrolled near Iran's waters. In January 2012 a Canadian warship departed to the Mediterranean Sea, according to the *Ottawa Citizen*, "for at least one year to provide a persistent Canadian presence near potential flashpoints." Six months later *HMCS Regina* was also dispatched to the region to join the growing US military presence off Iran's coast. The *National Post* reported: "Having the Charlottetown and other Canadian warships near Iran fits with the Harper government's strong opposition to Iran's suspected plan to acquire nuclear weapons."A number of media reports in 2008 described Canadian naval vessels running provocative manoeuvres off Iran's coast. "About 800 Canadian sailors are patrolling the politically turbulent waters near Iran and Pakistan," noted the *National Post*. Another paper reported that *HMCS Charlottetown* was patrolling 1,500 metres from Iranian territorial waters as part of a 50-ship armada under the *USS Harry Truman* carrier strike group. In July of that year, a *National Post* reporter on board a Canadian naval vessel explained: "The usual tense games were played this weekend as this Canadian warship responsible for refuelling and replenishing a coalition task force in the Indian Ocean passed in a heavy haze through one of the world's most dangerous flashpoints. Iranian radio operators trying to hail

the [Canadian vessel] Protecteur were interrupted by Omanis who firmly told their neighbours not speak to the Canadians who were making an 'innocent passage' through Omani territorial waters."

Canada, the US and our allies can patrol the international waters near Iran but when that country's navy does the same Conservative officials claim it is provocative. When the Iranian military began exercises near the mouth of the Persian Gulf at the start of 2012 minister Baird told the *Toronto Sun*: "Obviously I don't think any of us are surprised at any of the recent actions they are taking. We believe Iran constitutes the greatest threat to peace and security in the world." At times Canadian words have been quite menacing. In a February 2010 *Toronto Star* article headlined "Military action against Iran still on the table, Kent says" the junior foreign minister explained: "It's a matter of timing and it's a matter of how long we can wait without taking more serious pre-emptive action." "Pre-emptive action" is a euphemism for a large-scale US/Israeli bombing campaign. In March 2012 defence minister MacKay said the military was preparing for a possible war with Iran. "We are pursuing every diplomatic means, but the fact remains we have to be prepared for what may come and that's something the national defence department takes very seriously," MacKay told *Sun News*. "We are always planning, always preparing."

The Conservatives also tried to create the impression that Iran was preparing to attack Israel. During an early 2012 visit to Israel Baird compared the situation with Iran to the Nazi holocaust. "Obviously you can understand why the Jewish people and why Israel would take [Ayatollah Ali Khamenei] seriously. Hitler wrote *Mein Kampf* more than a decade before he became Chancellor of Germany. And they take these issues pretty seriously here."

In a February 2010 *Shalom Life* article discussing Iran, junior foreign minister Peter Kent stated: "An attack on Israel would be considered an attack on Canada." Foreign minister Cannon made a similar statement in mid-2009: "A nuclear threat against Israel is a threat against us all."

The strange thing is that it is Israel that possesses nuclear weapons and threatens to attack Iran, not the other way around. While Ottawa considers Iran's nuclear energy program a major threat, Israel's 100 atomic bombs have not provoked similar condemnation. At a number of International Atomic Energy Agency (IAEA) meetings the Harper government abstained on votes asking Israel to place its nuclear weapons program under IAEA controls. In September 2009 Ottawa condemned as "unbalanced" an IAEA resolution calling on Israel to join the Nuclear Non-Proliferation Treaty and have its nuclear facilities inspected. The Conservatives tried to block the vote. Ultimately, 100 countries supported the resolution while Israel opposed it. Canada, India, Georgia and the US abstained. In September 2010 Bloomberg cited Canada as one of three countries that opposed an IAEA probe of Israel's nuclear facilities as part of an Arab-led effort to create a nuclear-weapons-free Middle East.

This was only part of the Conservatives' hypocrisy and double standards regarding Iran's nuclear energy program. Alongside the Bush administration's move to support India as a counterweight to China, in 2008 the Conservatives decided Canada no longer objected to India's atomic weapons program. "Canada has changed its policy on nuclear non-proliferation to accommodate India's entry into the club of countries that can trade openly in nuclear fuel and technology, despite its nuclear weapons programs," noted the *Globe and Mail*. In November 2008 Ottawa

signed an agreement to export nuclear reactors and energy to India, even though India refused to sign the Nuclear Non-Proliferation Treaty. International Trade Minister Stockwell Day "accompanied by top executives from Atomic Energy of Canada Ltd., the crown corporation that designs nuclear reactors; nuclear engineering firm SNC-Lavalin Nuclear; and Cameco Corp., the Saskatoon-based uranium supplier," visited India in January 2009. The *Globe and Mail* quoted Day saying: "India recognizes that Canada was one of the significant voices in terms of seeing some of the past restrictions which have been placed on India lifted when it comes to civilian nuclear production. And we think we're going to be in a good position to make [the] pitch on the benefits of going with Canadian technology and Canadian supply."

US and Israeli officials have been claiming Iran is on the cusp of producing nuclear weapons for decades. An April 24, 1984, United Press International article headlined "'Ayatollah' Bomb in Production for Iran" warned that Iran was moving "very quickly" towards a nuclear weapon. Three years later the *Washington Post* published an article titled "Atomic Ayatollahs: Just What the Mideast Needs – an Iranian Bomb." At different points in the 1990s, noted Robert Fisk in January 2012, Israeli prime ministers Shimon Peres and Benjamin Netanyahu both said Iran would build a nuclear bomb by the end of that decade.

The double standards and power imbalance in the conflict between Israel/US and Iran are staggering. Iran has no atomic bomb while Israel has over 100 and the US has 5,000 nuclear warheads. The Carnegie Endowment for International Peace concluded in 2011 that Washington devotes more money to nuclear weapons than the rest of the world combined. At just over $60 billion a year, this is more than four times Iran's entire military budget.

The decision-makers in Washington and Tel Aviv are not threatened by Iranian nuclear weapons. Rather they worry about Iran's challenge to their regional domination. And, like a good follower, Harper has enthusiastically gone along with his friends.

7. Becoming a Warrior Nation

"If you want to be taken seriously in the world, you need the capacity to act — it's that simple."

Stephen Harper May 2008

"Strength is not an option; it is a vital necessity."

Stephen Harper June 2011

From Afghanistan to Libya to Lebanon and Iran, Harper's Conservatives have talked the warrior talk. They have also put our money where their mouth is.

Despite the beliefs of some, Canada has long been an important middle power, but the Conservatives have further militarized this country's foreign policy. Military spending is 2.3 percent higher than at the peak of the Cold War in 1952-53 and 26 percent greater than when the Berlin Wall came down. The Department of National Defence (DND) budget increased from $15 billion in 2005 to $23 billion in 2012 and the Conservatives plan to steadily increase the annual outlay to over $30-billion by 2027-28. According to Institut de recherche et d'informations socio- économiques, 6.4 percent of the government's budget went to the military in 2005. By 2012 that percentage had increased to 7.9 percent. Of the four G8 nations that are not permanent UN Security Council members – Canada, Germany, Italy and Japan – this country devoted the largest percentage of its GDP to the military at 1.6 percent versus 1.3 percent for the other three countries.

As part of the Canada First Defence Strategy, in mid-2008 the Conservatives announced a multi-decade plan to spend

$490 billion on military procurement. A year later they put aside $5 billion for land combat vehicles and decided to spend upwards of $30 billion on 65 F-35 stealth fighters. In 2011 the navy began a $33-billion shipbuilding program.

During the Conservatives first six years in office the military increased its numbers by a quarter and in 2012 the Canadian Forces had 68,000 regular soldiers and 27,000 reserves. Special forces grew particularly fast. In 2006 the military created the Special Operations Command to oversee a special operations aviation squadron and an expanded nuclear, biological, chemical and radiological response unit. The Special Operations Command is also responsible for the Special Operations Regiment, which began in September 2006 and was expected to reach 750 soldiers. Its members receive similar training to Joint Task Force 2 (JTF2) commandos. After having doubled from 300 to 600 men, in 2012 JTF2 was set to move to a 400-acre compound near Trenton Ontario at a cost of $350 million.

The Conservatives have supported special forces because these troops work closely with their US counterparts. The government is not required to divulge information about special forces operations so Ottawa can deploy these troops abroad and the public is none the wiser ("deniability" is the term sometimes used). Did the government dispatch JTF2 to Libya in contravention of UN Security Council resolution 1973? Were JTF2 members still fighting in Afghanistan after Harper promised to withdraw in 2011? In both instances the media reported as much but the information can't be confirmed since the public is only allowed to know what the government wants to tell us about their operations.

Canadian special forces began training the Jamaican Defence Force in 2008. Brigadier General Denis Thompson, head

of the Special Operations Forces Command, told the *Toronto Star* his soldiers contributed indirectly to the June 2010 capture of Jamaican gang leader Christopher Dudus Coke. Thompson said little about the 70 plus people — civilians and security forces — killed so Washington could imprison this reputed drug dealer (who apparently reinvested some of his ill-gotten funds into one of Kingston's poorest neighbourhoods).

Canadian special forces also trained their West African counterparts. Fifteen Canadian soldiers participated in Exercise Flintlock in Senegal and Mali in 2011. A December 2011 *Toronto Star* story reported: "The training efforts are closely tied to the larger US special forces efforts across the [Sahel] region" of northern Africa from Senegal to Sudan. In March 2012 a follow up training mission was cancelled because Mali's military was aggressively fighting a rebellion by largely nomadic Tuaregs in the north of the country. The *Ottawa Citizen*'s David Pugliese explained: "There was a debate in US military circles on whether to proceed with the Flintlock exercise, as a show of force that western nations are committed to supporting governments in the region. But it was decided that since Malian troops were so heavily involved in combat, its military couldn't spare the soldiers to be trained by Canadian and other special forces."

Canadian officials generally tell the media the aim of training other militaries is to help fight terror or the illicit drug trade. There are usually broader geopolitical motivations as well. According to its directorate, Canada's Military Training Assistance Program serves to "promote Canadian foreign and defence policy interests" through "the mechanism of military training assistance to develop and enhance bilateral and defence relationships with countries of strategic interest to Canada." As quoted in *Imperialist*

Canada the military further explains: "MTAP - trained countries are likely to cooperate with, and offer the Canadian forces access to their country and their forces, when necessary."

These training efforts were only part of the Conservatives' more forward international military posture. In November 2011 MacDonald, Dettwiler and Associates received a $30 million contract from the DND "for a surveillance solution capable of being rapidly deployed to any area of interest around the world." Similarly, the Canadian military intends to spend one billion dollars on unmanned aerial vehicles. According to an August 2012 *Ottawa Citizen* story, planning for the purchase of these armed drones began in the midst of NATO's 2011 bombing of Libya. The Conservatives also strengthened the Communications Security Establishment Canada (CSE), military spies focused on foreign signals intelligence. In explaining a $22 million increase to the CSE's 2009 budget, defence minister MacKay said: "Canada relies on this agency to provide foreign intelligence, advice and guidance vital to protecting electronic information in this country." Between 2001 and 2012 the number of CSE officers increased from 900 to 1,950 and at the same time its budget tripled to $400 million. To accommodate this growth, in early 2011 the government began building an $880 million, 72,000 square metre office connected to the CSIS headquarters in Ottawa.

The starkest example of the Conservatives' forward military strategy came to light in June 2011 when *Le Devoir* revealed negotiations to set up permanent bases in as many as seven countries. At that time the Conservatives had entered base agreements with Kuwait, Jamaica and Germany and looked to negotiate with Singapore, South Korea, Tanzania, Senegal and Kenya. "When the collection of operational support hubs

is complete," the *Toronto Star* reported a year later, "Canada's military will also have a permanent footprint in the Latin America and Caribbean region, on both sides of the African continent, in the swath of countries marked by the conflicts in Afghanistan and Pakistan, as well as in Southeast Asia."

Dubbed Operational Support Hub, the goal is to house equipment and soldiers overseas so the Canadian Forces can deploy more quickly. According to a military briefing note obtained by Postmedia, the bases are designed to improve the Canadian Forces' "ability to project combat power/security assistance and Canadian influence rapidly and flexibly anywhere in the world." Publicly, defence minister Peter MacKay called the base initiative part of expanding "our capability for expeditionary participation in international missions. ... We are big players in NATO. We're a country that has become a go-to nation in response to situations like what we're seeing in Libya, what we saw in Haiti."

Apparently, not every government approached was enamoured by Canada's military presence. According to documents unearthed by the *Toronto Star*, Canadian officials ran into difficulties when they asked an East African government — either Kenya or Tanzania — about hosting a military hub. "Local officials were suspicious and demanded to know Ottawa's motivation for moving into the region," noted the newspaper.

As part of this country's more forward military posture the head of the military publicly demanded a new war in July 2012. "We have some men and women who have had two, three and four tours and what they're telling me is 'Sir, we've got that bumper sticker. Can we go somewhere else now?'" General Walter Natynczyk told Canadian Press. "You also have the young sailors, soldiers, airmen and women who have just finished basic training

and they want to go somewhere and in their minds it was going to be Afghanistan. So if not Afghanistan, where's it going to be? They all want to serve."

It is not surprising that the head of the military would want to go to war (that's his job after all). What's troubling is that Natynczyk felt comfortable saying so in public and that neither the opposition parties nor any mainstream commentators criticized his call to arms. The Chief of the Defence Staff's warmongering is the logical outgrowth of the Conservatives bid to make Canadian society more militaristic.

By setting up overseas bases and increasing the military's size, the Conservatives are preparing for future wars. They're also building the ideological and cultural foundation for constant war. After waging war in Libya the Conservatives organized an $850,000 nationally televised celebration for Canada's "military heroes", which included flyovers from a dozen military aircraft. Harper told the 300 military personnel brought in from four bases: "We are celebrating a great military success ... Soldier for soldier, sailor for sailor, airman for airman, the Canadian Armed Forces are the best in the world."

As part of his push to define Canada as a warrior nation, at the June 2011 Conservative convention Harper mentioned "courageous warrior" as a founding Canadian principle. Asked to explain this position by *Maclean's* editor Kenneth White the prime minister cited Canada's role in fighting fascism and the Cold War. "The real defining moments for the country and for the world are those big conflicts where everything is at stake and where you take a side and show you can contribute to the right side." Asked whether we are in a great conflict or heading towards one Harper responded: "I think we always are."

The Conservatives' militarism is unrelenting. Harper made a surprise visit to a forward combat zone and on another occasion he got the military to give him a salute normally reserved for the governor-general. The updated 2011 citizenship handbook *Discover Canada: the Rights and Responsibilities of Citizenship* praises this country's military history. It includes more than a dozen photos of armed forces personnel, which is many more than the previous edition of the manual. Citizenship and Immigration Canada also decreed that citizenship ceremonies include a military speaker to promote the armed service. Introduced at the start of the ceremony, the veteran should declare: "As a Canadian citizen, you live in a democratic country where individual rights and freedoms are respected. Thousands of brave Canadians have fought and died for these rights and freedoms. The commitment to Canada of our men and women in uniform should never be forgotten."

Since 2006 the military has spent huge sums on a public relations campaign dubbed Operation Connection. "The purpose of Op CONNECTION is to showcase the men, women and equipment of the CF and to raise public awareness about the roles, capabilities and missions of the CF", notes the official description. "Op CONNECTION takes place throughout the year across Canada and events include Canada Day festivities across the country, the Calgary Stampede, the Canadian National Exhibition in Toronto, the Grand Prix de Trois-Rivieres, the NASCAR races in Montréal, the Santa Claus Parade in Yellowknife, Aboriginal Veterans Day in Northern Ontario, as well as others." During the 2011 Grey Cup football ceremony, for instance, CF-18 fighter jets roared over downtown Vancouver. Similarly, soldiers regularly appeared at NHL games rappelling down from the rafters or in sombre moments of silence for the fallen. When the Jets hockey

franchise returned to Winnipeg in 2011 their new logo was created in consultation with the Canadian Forces. "The design cues for the plane were inspired by the military jets flown by the Air Force over the years," the team said in a statement. In exchange for the logo design the team agreed to pay $1 million to military charities over 10 years.

Canadian militarists are increasingly bold. In December 2011 the Senate standing committee on national security and defence recommended re-establishing a training program that was offered at Canadian universities from 1912 until 1968. According to Lee Windsor, deputy director of the University of New Brunswick's Gregg Centre for the Study of War and Society, the Canadian Officers Training Corps program "introduced university undergraduates to a form of military service on campus, providing them with leadership and other military training and preparing them to join the reserve or the regular force if they wished to do so." The University of Alberta agreed to host a trial program.

Five years into the Conservative government the Canadian Forces openly proclaimed that it should determine public opinion. In November 2011 *Embassy* reported: "An annual report from the Department of National Defence says Canadians should appreciate that their values are shaped in part by their military. That represents a shift from past annual departmental reports that said departmental activities were informed by Canadian interests and values. Now it's the other way around."

In introducing their new "Canadian identity" program, the military report says its goal is to make sure "Canadians are aware of, understand, and appreciate the history, proficiency, and values of the Canadian military as part of Canada's identity." Incredibly, reports *Embassy*, the Canadian Forces admit to having

spent $353.6 million and directed 661 staff members to carrying out these public relations efforts in 2010-11.

The military's efforts also spurred various private initiatives. At the end of 2011 a group began selling Heroes Force, a GI Joe style Canadian action figure depicting airforce, army and navy personnel. The second edition of the dolls included a JTF2 special commando replica.

Begun in 2008 the True Patriot Love Foundation raised $10 million for soldiers' causes while the Canadian Hero Fund scholarship program gave millions more to the children of fallen soldiers. A number of universities signed on to the Hero Fund program, which was pushed by the former head of the military Rick Hillier. In a similar initiative in November 2011 the University of New Brunswick and Université de Moncton established "supportive employment and academic policies for members of Canada's Reserve Force." At about the same time the International Brotherhood of Boilermakers joined the Helmets to Hard Hats initiative. Modeled after an American program of the same name, the Conservative-backed initiative gives veterans, reservists and current soldiers priority access to jobs and training opportunities in the trades. During the launch of the project at the Boilermakers hall in Edmonton, Harper said the building trades were a "natural fit" for many former military. "If you can drive a tank, why not drive a bulldozer. If you can drive a LAV, why not drive a Kenworth. Forklifts work the same everywhere and so do backhoes."

Unions were joined by the media in promoting militaristic celebrations. On November 11, 2011, the *Ottawa Citizen* set up a Twitter account "Wearethedead" to recite the names of every Canadian Forces member killed at war. They are tweeting the name and a brief description of a deceased soldier each hour of

every day, which will take more than 13 years. The *Citizen*'s managing editor Andrew Potter explained: "Through this Twitter account, and through more extensive use of social media down the line, we hope to make the act of keeping faith a more subtle, but in many ways more permanent feature, of the lives of Canadians."

The growth in militarism and 'support the troops' efforts spurred an extreme, at times paranoid, mindset. In June 2009 a Barrie, Ontario radio station called on listeners to complain that military supplier CANEX forbid its employees from wearing red as part of Red Friday support the troops days. Apparently, the story was based on hearsay but the company's employees were immediately issued red shirts adorned with a "Support the Troops" logo. In an even more scary sign of a growing 'my country right or wrong' attitude, 16 University of Regina professors were viciously attacked for criticizing the school's Project Hero scholarship program, which makes university free and provides a \$1,000 annual stipend to "dependents of Canadian Forces personnel deceased while serving with an active mission." In March 2010 the professors released a statement opposing the program's "unquestioning glorification of military action", prompting a political and media firestorm that included criticism from Conservative MPs and Saskatchewan Premier Brad Wall.

Beyond the chill factor, efforts to promote the military had mixed success. According to a 2011 DND assessment, 87 percent of Canadians "feel that the [CF] is a source of pride." The military took this as a sign that their \$350 million outreach campaign was successful. Reality is slightly more complicated. While there is widespread support for the institution, most Canadians still rank the military low on their list of political concerns. A May 2011 Environics poll found that the top priority of 29 percent of

Canadians was the economy/job creation, 13 percent cited health care, six percent pointed to deficit reduction while defence was down the list with only four percent calling it their top priority. Furthermore, most Canadians don't want the military to focus on war making. A mid-2011 Ipsos-Reid poll released to military leaders suggested that most Canadians want the Canadian Forces to prioritize initiatives closer to home and a December 2010 poll of 1,043 Canadians found that the population preferred the military focus on disaster relief in local communities, search and rescue, patrolling Canada's air space, land and maritime areas as well as enforcing Arctic sovereignty. Fighting the war on terrorism was at the bottom of the list.

The element of Harper's militarism with the least popular support was likely the Conservatives ambivalence towards international arms control measures. They ended both the special fund on landmines and the position of Landmines Ambassador, while CIDA stopped including mine action as a core part of its development agenda. After six years as Foreign Affairs' senior coordinator for mine action, Earl Turcotte resigned in February 2011 to protest the government's position on the Convention on Cluster Munitions. Turcotte was unhappy about the ratification conditions the Conservatives added to the convention to allow Canada to participate in joint military operations with countries that refused to sign it (notably the US). "It falls way below even the minimum threshold of legality under international humanitarian law and is an insult to colleagues in other countries who, seemingly unlike Canada, have negotiated in good faith," Turcotte told the *Toronto Star* in April 2012. "Most tragically, it will make Canada complicit in the use of a weapon that for good reason we have supposedly banned. Having led the delegation I

can say that without a doubt this legislation is the worst of any of the 111 countries that have so far ratified the treaty." Former Australian Prime Minister John Fraser also criticized the move in June 2012. "It is a pity the current Canadian government, in relation to cluster munitions, does not provide any real lead to the world. Its approach is timid, inadequate and regressive." The director of the Cluster Munition Coalition, Laura Cheeseman, was even more forthright. "Canada cannot claim to have banned cluster bombs when it proposes to allow its military to help others use the weapons, and even leaves open the possibility of Canadian forces using them."

Through access to information CBC News discovered that the foreign minister's office made civil servants invite Steve Torino, president of the Canadian Shooting Sports Association, to a July 2011 Arms Trade Treaty meeting at the UN. Torino was supposed "to advise the Government of Canada on any potential implications of an Arms Trade Treaty for Canadian firearms owners." The minister's office also ordered last-minute changes to Canada's position on the Arms Trade Treaty, which was designed to limit weapons from getting into conflict zones or into the hands of human rights violators. The Canadian delegation recommended the treaty not include "recreational" weapons. The Conservatives position at the 2011 negotiations, which referred to the chair's draft text as "too ambitious" and "seeking too much", prompted immediate opposition from at least 10 member countries. For its part, Amnesty International launched a campaign claiming the global banana trade was better regulated than the arms market.

The Conservatives continued to obstruct the treaty during the final round of Arms Trade Treaty negotiations. In an overwhelmingly negative speech to the UN in July 2012 a Foreign

Affairs deputy director, Habib Massoud, laid out the Conservatives' position. Taking a position that put Canada offside with the bulk of the international community, Massoud called for the proposed arms tracking secretariat to be "minimal, small, and flexible" and financed entirely through existing UN budgets. "In Canada's view, detailed reporting about each and every [arms] transaction can, in certain circumstances, be both impractical and unrealistic. The sheer volume of such transactions would overwhelm virtually any administrative system now in existence." An internal government position paper, released through an access to information request, put it more pointedly. "Canada does not support mandatory reporting on ammunition, parts and components, as well as technology and equipment transfers."

Despite substantial growth in internationally focused private security companies, the Conservatives have failed to regulate the industry. In Canada these companies, including Montréal-based GuardaWorld with 8,000 employees in conflict zones, are treated no differently than other transnational corporations. Unlike some other jurisdictions, Canadian private security companies face no controls on professional background, criminal history, humanitarian training etc.

The Conservatives have ignored or weakened arms control measures and made it more difficult for concerned Canadians to challenge the industry. Richard Sanders, coordinator of the Coalition to Oppose the Arms Trade, explained: "Finally, after years of delays and just a few hours after Japan's horrifying earthquake on March 11 [2011], the Harper government finally released its latest deeply-flawed report on Canada's military exports between 2007 and 2009. This timing ensured that the latest data on Canada's participation in the international weapons

trade was conveniently buried beneath a tsunami of news about Japan's natural catastrophe." The government also omitted or ignored a great deal of sales. The Canadian Association of Defence and Security Industries claims its members exported some $15 billion in "defence" and "security" products from 2007 to 2009 yet the government's report accounted for $1.5 billion during that period (as per usual sales to the US were not detailed). Project Ploughshares senior program officer Ken Epps criticized the failure to fully account for weapons sales. "In a highly connected, digital age when it is possible to track people and packages across the planet in real-time one would be forgiven for thinking that Canadian officials should be able at leisure to monitor military exports and report their value. Not so."

In another sop to arms manufacturers, the Conservatives expanded the list of countries eligible to receive Canadian automatic weapons. In April 2008 Canada's Automatic Firearms Country Control List was increased from 20 to 31 states. In doing so the government pointed to "the valuable contributions that Canada's defence industry makes to the nation's prosperity."

The Conservatives helped military companies in numerous other ways. They directly supported the arms industry's main lobby group. Foreign Affairs' website explained: "To help Canadian firms navigate these complexities [regulations on arms sales] and overcome key challenges in their export markets, the Trade Commissioner Service (TCS) is embedding a trade commissioner in the Canadian Association of Defence and Security Industries (CADSI)." In August 2011 this industry association received a $149,000 grant under the government's Global Opportunities for Associations program. CADSI also benefited from direct political support. In December 2011 senior

representatives from DND, the Canadian Forces, Foreign Affairs and the Canadian Commercial Corporation (CCC) participated in a CADSI trade mission to Kuwait. According to the official press release, they "discussed with Kuwaiti government and military leaders how Canadian and Kuwaiti businesses in the defence and security sector can work together effectively in Kuwait and more generally in the Gulf." CADSI president Tim Page applauded what he described as the Conservatives "whole of government effort" with the Kuwaiti monarchy. "We believe this is a good example of how defence spending in Canada can be leveraged to achieve international business success. We hope this will be the start of similar initiatives that bring Canada's defence and security industries together with the Canadian government and military in markets of strategic interest to Canada." CADSI's costs for the mission were partly covered by the Global Opportunities for Associations program. The government-backed corporate lobby group also led trade missions to Saudi Arabia and the UAE.

During the Harper reign the CCC, whose board is appointed by the government, has taken on a more expansive role as a go-between on military sales with foreign governments. According to a June 2011 *Embassy* article, "the Canadian Commercial Corporation has been transformed from a low-profile Canadian intermediary agency to a major player in promoting Canadian global arms sales." Traditionally, the CCC sold Canadian weaponry to the US Department of Defense under the 1956 Defence Production Sharing Agreement but during the Conservative government it began emulating some aspects of the US defence department's Foreign Military Sales program, which facilitates that country's global arms sales. In June 2012 *Embassy* noted: "In the last few years, the Canadian Commercial Corporation, a

Crown corporation, has helped Canadian firms sell everything from military hardware and weapons to wiretapping technology, forensics for ballistics, surveillance, document detection, sensor systems, bulletproof vests and helmets, training, and other services." According to CCC president Marc Whittingham, who wrote in a May 2010 issue of *Hill Times* that "there is no better trade show for defence equipment than a military mission", the agency is "partnering with government ministers to get the job done."

In 2007 the Conservatives established a multi-million dollar subsidy program for weapons and aerospace companies known as the Strategic Aerospace and Defence Initiative and during the 2008/09 economic downturn the Conservatives turned to the military to stimulate the economy. A March 2009 *Edmonton Journal* headline noted: "Tories fight recession with military spending." During a cross-country tour to announce various public works on military bases, minister MacKay called the contracts "an important part of the government's effort to stimulate the economy."

Reacting to these initiatives, the Canadian Peace Congress complained: "The Harper policy of the rapid militarization of the economy is the only job creation project the government has to offer the youth, the unemployed and the underemployed." This statement was disturbingly prescient. Wikileaks revealed that Conservative Parliamentary Secretary for Defence Laurie Hawn told US officials he hoped the rising number of unemployed would increase military enrolment: "He [Hawn] expressed the hope that rising unemployment rates at home on one hand, and the welcome new deployment of US troops in Kandahar on the other, would help the Canadian Forces to recruit and retain troops," explained a March 2009 cable from the US embassy.

Beyond short-term stimulus, military spending props up important components of Canadian industry. Many shipyards, airplane manufacturers and high-tech companies depend on military contracts. In 2011 the Conservatives announced a $33 billion 30-year naval contract with Irving and Seaspan shipyards. A *CBC.ca* headline at the time noted: "Shipbuilding deals will stabilize industry, Harper says". Tom Ring, an assistant deputy minister at Public Works and Government Services Canada, wrote in March 2012: "Canada's shipbuilding industry is now on the cusp of resurgence thanks to the federal government's National Shipbuilding Procurement Strategy." Alongside the multi-billion dollar shipbuilding industry, aerospace companies such as CAE, Bombardier and Héroux-Devtek benefit from military spending. With this country home to the fifth largest aerospace industry in the world, the Aerospace Industries Association of Canada (AIAC) was a strong proponent of the Conservatives' plan to purchase 65 F-35 fighter jets. "AIAC is committed to the competitiveness of the Canadian aerospace industry and, as such, to the optimization and assessment of the economic benefits related to the government's decision to procure the Joint Strike Fighter F-35 for our Forces," said Claude Lajeunesse, president of AIAC in March 2011. In April 2012 the *Toronto Star* reported: "The F-35 jet has been the whipping boy for auditors and politicians all week, but it remains the darling of Canada's aerospace industry" with over 70 Canadian companies already building parts on contracts expected to be worth billions over the course of the plane's production run.

Even beyond the shipbuilding and aerospace industries the self-identified military industry is large. The Canadian Association of Defence and Security Industries (CADSI), representing 860 companies, claimed they did $12.6 billion in business in 2011.

Hundreds of Canadian companies produce products ranging from bullets to armoured vehicles. The Federation of American Scientists Arms Sales Monitoring Project ranked Canada number six in foreign military sales deliveries in 2009 while another group concluded that Canada was the tenth largest exporter of small arms and light weapons in 2007.

Most of the world's biggest weapons companies have a Canadian subsidiary because this allows them to access subsidies made available by Ottawa and it also improves their chances of winning contracts with the Canadian military. Many Canadian-based military suppliers have US subsidiaries for the same reasons. These companies include CAE, Bombardier and less known corporations such as Atlantis Systems. In 2011 Atlantis Systems' US subsidiary, Atlantis Systems America, qualified for the US Army Program Executive Office for Simulation, Training and Instrumentation, which allows them to bid on $17.5 billion in contracts.

As outlined above, the Conservatives' militarism is motivated by economic, ideological and cultural forces, but it also reflects direct personal ties as well. Prior to entering government, Harper's first defence minister, Gordon O'Connor, lobbied for military suppliers such as BAE systems, United Defense and Airbus Military. Similarly, the Conservatives chose Derek Burney, the former head of CAE, to oversee the transfer of power from Paul Martin's Liberals. Burney now chairs the International Advisory Board of GardaWorld, a leading private security company. Nigel Wright, Harper's chief of staff at the time of publication, previously directed Hawker Beechcraft, a partner of US military giant Lockheed Martin. Listed among *Embassy's* 80 most influential foreign policy decision-makers, Wright was on leave from Onex, the company that bought Hawker.

The personal ties to military companies go both ways. Conservative allies in the Canadian Forces and DND used their public sector careers as a springboard to lucrative defence industry positions. After he retired as head of the military in 2008 Rick Hillier took a position on the advisory board of Provincial Aerospace and became a "strategic advisor" for MacDonald Dettwiler and Associates (alongside former Harper advisor Tom Flanagan). In October 2011 CGI Group, a provider of information technology and business process services, appointed 12-year DND veteran Ken Taylor vice-president of Cybersecurity Canada. A CGI Group press release noted: "In his new role, Ken will work closely with both government and commercial clients as part of the newly formed Canadian Defence, Public Safety and Intelligence business unit under the leadership of Lieutenant-General (retired) Andrew Leslie." Three weeks after Leslie retired as chief of transformation for the Canadian Forces in September 2011 CGI Group appointed him to lead this unit. The Ottawa-based business unit will "serve the Canadian Forces around the globe."

All Canadians should worry, as former US president Dwight Eisenhower warned, that the influence of the military-industrial complex will grow to the point where democracy is imperiled. Can anyone argue that it can't happen here?

8. Consequences of Militarism

As Harper's Conservatives continue to promote Canadian militarism how will this country change? We can look south of our border to see the consequences of a society dominated by the military industrial complex. But we can also look at Canada's experience in Afghanistan to see what happens when military concerns outweigh all others.

The Conservatives repeatedly lied about Canada's role in Afghanistan. They deceived Canadians about prisoner abuse, development aid and the reason for fighting. Harper also hoodwinked most Canadians about extending Canada's military engagement into its second decade. With public opinion increasingly hostile to the occupation of Afghanistan, the Conservatives voted for a 2008 House of Commons resolution calling for Canada's combat mission to end by July 2011. During the Fall 2008 election campaign Harper said: "We're planning our withdrawal of Canadian troops from Afghanistan in 2011. At that point, the mission ... as we've known it, we intend to end it." In a bid to demobilize the anti-war movement and keep the issue off the political agenda, the minority Conservative government regularly reiterated this commitment. In an end of 2009 interview the prime minister claimed: "[After 2011] we will not be undertaking any activities that require any kind of military presence, other than the odd guard guarding an embassy." Eight months later the Prime Minister's Office emailed a memorandum to reporters declaring: "We just want to be absolutely clear that Canada's military mission in Afghanistan ends in 2011." Six months before the publicly announced withdrawal date the Conservatives claimed they had a

change of mind, deciding to maintain up to a thousand troops until 2014. Notwithstanding their deceptive comments, it had long been clear to those paying close attention that they did not plan to end the military mission in 2011. Already in November 2008 Canwest reported: "[Peter] McKay hinted that Canadian troops might still have a role to play in Afghanistan after 2011 — the deadline set by Parliament for the end of the current combat mission." Two months earlier the *Ottawa Citizen* reported that Canada's Afghanistan Procurement Task Force "is pushing ahead with its plan to buy aerial drones [by 2012] outfitted with weapons even as the Harper government is promising to pull troops out of Afghanistan in 2011." In the *Black Book of Canadian Foreign Policy*, which was printed at the start of 2009, I wrote: "As this book went to press, Ottawa appeared set to steadily increase the number of troops to 4,000 for the 2009 Afghan elections and then draw down to 1,000 soldiers after 2011." This sentence was prescient and a similar plan may be in the works for after 2014. In February 2012 Major General Mike Day, the head of Canada's training contingent and the NATO officer in charge of building up Afghan security forces, told Postmedia: "We are going to continue post-2014, there are no ifs, ands, ors, or buts about that ... I read in the press, and it's frustrating, idiotic really, to say we are out of here by the end of 2014. That has never been the case and never will be the case. We will continue. What is true is that the mission will change and we have to prepare for that." Two months later Harper said: "Our plan at the current time is obviously for the mission that goes to 2014, but as we approach that date, we will examine all options and we will take the decision that's in the best interests of this country and in the best interests of our security objectives for the globe and not an ideological knee-jerk response like the NDP."

In other words, the Conservatives lied about their plans to maintain troops in Afghanistan after 2011. They also lied about consulting Parliament on extending the military's presence. "On the extension of the mission in Afghanistan, everybody used to agree that there had to be a vote in the House before there was an extension of the mission," NDP leader Jack Layton complained in November 2010 after the Conservatives refused to take a proposal for an extension to Parliament. "It was in the Conservative platform, it was in the throne speech." Then leader of the government in the House, John Baird, didn't deny it. "Our government has been very clear and the practice has been that if we are going to put troops into combat, to put them in a war situation and for the sake of legitimacy that we made a practice of bringing it before Parliament." But, partly to avoid a full parliamentary debate, the Conservatives described the military's post-2011 role as non-combat. Science and technology minister Gary Goodyear claimed that "it's not a military mission" to maintain a thousand troops in Afghanistan.

At the time of the extension, in November 2010, then-Liberal leader Michael Ignatieff asked: "Can the Prime Minister guarantee that this (new engagement) is not going to involve combat, that it is going to be out of Kandahar and that the training will occur in safe conditions in Kabul?" Harper replied: "The answer is yes to all those questions. ... As the minister of national defence, the minister of foreign affairs and others have said, we are looking at a non-combat mission that will occur. It will be a training mission that will occur in classrooms, behind the wire, in bases." Again, Harper deliberately misled the public. The bulk of Canadian troops remain active in a violent conflict and Canadian special forces continue to fight alongside their US counterparts.

In September 2011 the *Ottawa Citizen* reported: "Canadian military trainers helped defend a NATO compound in Kabul last week when insurgents launched a dramatic attack against the US Embassy and surrounding neighbourhood." Sixteen people were killed in the assault. After this attack Brigadier General Craig King told a parliamentary committee that Canadian "trainers" were spread over a dozen locations in Kabul, which he described as an "extremely violent" city. A month later a suicide bomber killed a Canadian soldier, prompting Harper to acknowledge the "significant risk" involved in the "training" mission.

The violent character of Canada's "training" was predictable. Former chief of defence Rick Hillier told *Maclean's* in October 2009: "If you try to help train and develop the Afghan army or police in ... Afghanistan, you are going to be in combat." If the Conservatives' aim were simply to train Afghan troops it would be safer and cheaper to bring them here. This country's Military Training Assistance Program brings over a 1,000 military personnel from dozens of southern countries to train in Canada every year. The main aim of Canada's training, the second-largest contribution to the NATO training mission, was to enable the US war effort. A March 2012 *Ottawa Citizen* headline explained: "Canadian training mission meant to free up US soldiers for Afghan combat: documents." According to briefing notes prepared for Governor General David Johnston's December 2011 visit to Afghanistan, 950 Canadian soldiers were deployed to Kabul and other Afghan cities to "free up American forces to move to a [more aggressive] combat role."

In all probability Canadian special forces also remain active in Afghanistan. Even though JTF2 was supposedly covered by the 2008 parliamentary vote to cease combat operations by

July 2011, they continued to fight. In January 2012 Matthew Fisher reported on a farewell banquet organized by the governor of Kandahar for departing Canadian officials. "Also at the dinner were members of [Canadian Brig.-Gen. Dean] Milner's leadership team, fresh troops from a US army battalion from Alaska — the Arctic Wolves — who were to take over Canada's battle space in a few days, and a dozen US Navy Seals, Special Forces Marines and *commandos from Canada's secretive JTF2, who had emerged from the desert after a clandestine mission*." (emphasis added) In April 2012 the *Ottawa Citizen* reported: "US and Canadian officials are in talks over a Pentagon request to keep Canadian special forces in Afghanistan beyond the 2014 withdrawal the Conservative government promised."

At the end of 2011 the Conservatives announced an agreement for Canadian troops to hand over captured Afghans to US forces. Considering the sensitivity of the detainee transfer issue (see below), it is unlikely the Conservatives would have negotiated such a deal if there were little or no chance Canadian troops would detain Afghans. "What I drew from this [agreement]", Amnesty Canada's lawyer Paul Champ told the Canadian Press, "was that Special Forces are still very active there. Canada decided we needed to come up with some new deal, and then after some further reflection they decided to make it public just in case it gets leaked in a year."

According to documents CBC News obtained through access to information, a JTF2 member said he felt his commanders "encouraged" them to commit war crimes. The soldier, whose name was not released, claimed a fellow JTF2 member shot an Afghan with his hands raised in the act of surrender. The allegations of wrongdoing were first made to his superior officers

177

in 2006 yet the military ombudsman didn't begin investigating until June 2008. The JTF2 member told the ombudsman's office "that although he reported what he witnessed to his chain of command, he does not believe they are investigating, and are being 'very nice to him.'" After a three and a half year investigation, the Canadian Forces National Investigation Service cleared the commanders in December 2011. But they failed to release details of the allegations, including who was involved or when and where it happened. The public was supposed to simply trust the National Investigation Service.

Allegations of JTF2 wrongdoing should be seen in the context of a violent war. In January 2012 a video emerged of four US Marines urinating on dead Afghans and two months later a US sergeant slaughtered 17 civilians, including nine children, in a drunken rage. Of course Canadian troops participated in their share of violence. In his 2010 book *A Line in the Sand: Canadians at War in Kandahar*, which included a foreword by Harper, Captain Ray Wiss, praised Canadian troops as "the best at killing people ... We are killing a lot more of them than they are of us, and we have been extraordinarily successful recently... For the past week, we have managed to kill between 10 and 20 Taliban every day." Apparently, Canadian special forces participated in highly unpopular nighttime assassination raids. The *Globe and Mail* reported in December 2008: "A top Canadian commander has defended his forces' night raids on Afghan homes after a leading human-rights group and the Kabul government condemned the controversial tactic." After describing an Afghanistan Independent Human Rights Commission report criticizing night-time assassination raids and the Canadian Forces' reaction to the report, the article noted: "the *Globe and Mail* is bound by an embedding agreement at Kandahar

Air Field that forbids detailing Special Forces operations."
Presumably this was the journalist's way of relaying special forces
operational information without being thrown off the base (as was
done to other reporters).

In addition to special forces and 950 military "trainers",
the Conservatives offloaded parts of the mission to private security
corporations. Planning for this began years earlier. In a December
2009 *Ottawa Citizen* article headlined "Canada preparing a
military role in Afghanistan beyond 2011, say experts" David
Pugliese reported that the military sent "two surveillance aircraft
to Afghanistan in a move some defence analysts see as laying
the groundwork for a military mission in Kandahar beyond the
announced 2011 pullout date." Pugliese discovered the plans when
the US army announced that a US company received a $12-million
contract to modify the two Canadian aircraft, which were expected
to come aboard in June 2011. According to a researcher with
the Canadian-American Strategic Review, these Intelligence,
Surveillance and Reconnaissance (ISR) aircraft were expected to
use private contractors so "it might be argued that ISR flights are
not directly related to combat." Stephen Priestley noted: "Seen in
that light, performing ISR over Kandahar would not be regarded as
an extension of the CF's combat mission."

In August 2010 Afghan president Hamid Karzai
announced a ban on security contractors. Harper immediately
criticized the move. "Ban on hired guns will complicate Afghan
exit: PM", noted a *CTV.ca* headline. "I will certainly concede
that President Karzai's recent decision will complicate some of
those choices in the future," the prime minister told reporters.
The Conservatives were worried partly because they hoped to
outsource some of the work undertaken by the Canadian Forces

to private security firms. In response to foreign pressure Karzai postponed the closing of private security firms until March 2012, which was then pushed back to September 2013.

According to documents released to Parliament in February 2012, over the four previous years Canada spent $41 million on 11 different security firms in Afghanistan. Private security was even used to protect the military's forward operating bases in Kandahar. Some of the firms the Canadian Forces hired, including Hart Security and Watan Risk Management, were implicated in previous abuses or were accused of employing Afghan warlords. Private security firms in Afghanistan operated under guidelines that practically guaranteed significant civilian casualties. After a Canadian officer was killed by a private security official in August 2008, Canadian Major Corey Frederickson told the *National Post* that the "normal contact drill [for private security] is that as soon as they get hit with something then it's 360 [degrees], open up on anything that moves." Describing the aftermath of the Canadian soldier's death, *Stars and Stripes* noted that "when questioned by Canadian and US military officers, several of the Afghan security guards freely admitted opening fire on what they thought were Taliban fighters. But when informed that a Canadian soldier had been wounded, their stories began to change, and many never claimed to have fired at all."

George Orwell would be impressed by the Conservatives' lies. He'd have been particularly impressed by their spin on the treatment of detainees transferred to the Afghan Army and National Directorate of Security (NDS). Harper's first defence minister Gordon O'Connor was forced to apologize for misleading parliament about the Canadian Forces' detainee transfer agreement. In May 2006 he told the House, "The Red Cross or the Red Crescent

is responsible to supervise their treatment once the prisoners are in the hands of the Afghan authorities. If there is something wrong with their treatment, the Red Cross or Red Crescent would inform us and we would take action." The Red Cross said it was not party to any monitoring agreement and rebuked the minister because the organization's representatives in Kandahar repeatedly tried to warn the Canadian army about prisoner abuse.

In May 2007 the Conservatives once again denied allegations that individuals detained by Canadians, and turned over to the Afghan army and prison system, were tortured. The denials contradicted the facts but the depth of the lie wasn't fully exposed until Richard Colvin, the second highest ranked Canadian diplomat in Afghanistan from 2006 to 2007, testified before a parliamentary committee in November 2009. "In early March 2007, I informed an interagency meeting of some 12 to 15 officials in Ottawa that, 'The NDS tortures people, that's what they do, and if we don't want our detainees tortured, we shouldn't give them to the NDS.' ... The response from the Canadian Expeditionary Force Command (CEFCOM) note-taker was to stop writing and put down her pen." At about the same time, diplomats in Afghanistan sending reports to Ottawa were ordered to withhold information that didn't promote "a happy face" about the handling of prisoners. The Conservatives feared that graphic reports about the treatment of detainees, even if censored, could be uncovered by the opposition parties or media through access-to-information laws.

After Colvin's testimony the Conservatives refused to heed the opposition's call for a public inquiry into the matter. Instead they doubled down. The day after Colvin spoke defence minister MacKay told the House: "There has not been a single,

181

solitary proven allegation of abuse involving a transferred Taliban prisoner by Canadian forces." On December 10, 2009, the opposition parties, which were then in the majority, passed a motion requiring that the government release all un-redacted documents concerning Afghan detainees to the committee hearing the issue. The government refused, which may have violated the constitution and put it in contempt of Parliament. On December 30, 2009, the prime minister "prorogued" (suspended) Parliament to prevent the parliamentary committee from continuing to probe the issue. Opposition MPs, reported *CBC.ca*, called this "move an 'almost despotic' attempt to muzzle parliamentarians amid controversy over the Afghan detainees affair."

Under the Geneva Conventions the military force that detains someone is responsible for their treatment and many of those detained by the Canadian Forces were likely tortured with power cables, knives, open flames or rape. The United Nations Human Rights Commission, the US State Department and Afghanistan's Independent Human Rights Commission all reported widespread torture in Afghanistan detention facilities. The latter group found that "torture and other cruel, inhuman or degrading treatment are common in the majority of law enforcement institutions, and at least 98.5 percent of interviewed victims have been tortured." Additionally, dozens of individuals given to the Afghan army by the Canadian Forces were unaccounted for, perhaps lost in a prison system that does not keep good records or maybe killed. Many of those the Canadian Forces detained likely had little to do with the Taliban. Richard Colvin reported to the special parliamentary committee: "It was the NDS that told us that many or most of our detainees were unconnected to the insurgency. This assessment was reported to Ottawa. The NDS also told us that, because the

intelligence value of Canadian-transferred detainees was so low, it did not want them."

The Canadian Forces regularly handed over children they suspected of Taliban ties to the NDS. According to a secret document released through access to information, on March 30, 2010, minister MacKay was briefed about juvenile detainees. To get a sense of what he learned one can go to an April 2010 UN report titled *Children and Armed Conflict* that explained: "The use of harsh interrogation techniques and forced confession of guilt by the Afghan Police and NDS was documented, including the use of electric shocks and beating [of kids]. ... Available information points to sexual violence as a widespread phenomenon." On June 2008 the *Toronto Star* reported that in late 2006 a Canadian soldier heard an Afghan soldier raping a young boy and later saw the boy's "lower intestines falling out of his body." Reportedly, the Canadian military police were told by their commanders not to interfere when Afghan soldiers and police sexually abused children.

For many Canadians and others around the world the war in Afghanistan came to symbolize a wanton disregard for human rights and international law. Part of this can be traced half way across the world to Guantanamo Bay Cuba where the US built a prison for "unlawful" Afghan combatants. The Conservatives supported this detention facility. After every other country repatriated their citizens detained in Guantanamo, Ottawa refused to call for Omar Khadr's release, who was detained in Afghanistan when he was only 15. The government sent Canadian agents to interrogate Khadr under the pretext of aiding him and then turned the contents of that interview over to the US. In so doing, the Conservatives violated Khadr's charter rights. In October 2010 Khadr accepted a deal to plead guilty to multiple charges on condition that he would

183

only serve one year of an eight-year sentence at Guantanamo. The Conservatives refused to allow Khadr to return and as this book went to print they continued to block him from serving out the remainder of his sentence in a Canadian jail.

Considering their treatment of Khadr it shouldn't come as a surprise that the Conservatives instructed the Canadian Security Intelligence Service to use information obtained through torture (previous policy was to discard intelligence that could be tainted). Privately, Public Safety Minister Vic Toews told CSIS to use any information if public safety was at stake and in February 2012 he told Parliament: "Information obtained by torture is always discounted. But the problem is, can one safely ignore it when Canadian lives and property are at stake?"

The Conservatives also lied about the humanitarian side of the mission in Afghanistan. In November 2011 the chairwoman of the Senate national security and defence committee and member of the Independent Panel on Afghanistan, Pamela Wallin, wrote in the *National Post*: "We have also built some 44 schools where nearly eight million young Afghans are finally able to learn the basics. And nearly one-third of these students are girls." In a *Defence Watch* blog titled "Conservative Senator Pamela Wallin's Afghanistan Spin Reaches New Heights" David Pugliese noted: "That's quite a statement. And absolutely not true. Think of it – eight million kids taught in 44 schools (which have been constructed since 2008). Those are some big schools. But it's not the first time that government officials have made misleading statements on the Afghan mission, in particular the Kandahar school situation."

A Canadian Press investigation found only 19,000 students enrolled at Canadian-built schools and most of them were boys. One Canadian-funded school — Shaheed Sardar

Mohammad Dawood — visited by the Canadian Press had no students. "With nothing to do, four teachers in their early twenties sat in the principal's office sipping sweet chai tea and eating small cakes," the news agency reported. "It was quiet in the room, but children could be heard playing in the streets beyond the school's fenced front yard."

Despite Conservative claims, the war in Afghanistan wasn't about improving women's rights. Canadian officials ignored or downplayed the misogynistic policies pursued by President Hamid Karzai. In early 2012 the notoriously corrupt president backed a decree claiming women are worth less than men. "Men are fundamental and women are secondary," noted the statement by a government-sponsored group of religious leaders known as the Ulema Council. "Women are subordinate to men, should not mix in work or education and must always have a male guardian when they travel."

How can you tell when the Canadian military and their supporters are lying about a war? When they know a reporter is present.

9. Business Above All Else

As outlined so far the two main themes of Harper's foreign policy are growing militarism and support for corporate interests above all others. The latter issue was discussed in the first two chapters and we return to the role of big business here. While corporate interests have long dominated this country's foreign affairs the Harper government is unflinching in its corporate orientation. This is best seen in Latin America, in international trade agreements and in pushing a product that kills.

Stopping social change in Latin America

Anyone who has studied the past century of imperialism in Latin America knows that the coup has been a primary tool of foreign interference in this region Washington considers its backyard. As such, it is appropriate to begin this story of Canada's role in Latin America by discussing the most recent coups.

On June 22, 2012, the left-leaning president of Paraguay, Fernando Lugo, was ousted in what some called an "institutional coup". Upset with Lugo for disrupting 61-years of one party rule, Paraguay's ruling class claimed he was responsible for a murky incident that left 17 peasants and police dead and the senate voted to impeach the president. The vast majority of countries in the hemisphere refused to recognize the new government. The Union of South American Nations (UNASUR) suspended Paraguay's membership after Lugo's ouster, as did the MERCOSUR trading bloc. In early August the Council on Hemispheric Affairs reported: "Not a single Latin American government has recognized [Federico] Franco's presidency."

But Canada was one of only a handful of countries in the world that immediately recognized the new government. "Canada notes that Fernando Lugo has accepted the decision of the Paraguayan Senate to impeach him and that a new president, Federico Franco, has been sworn in," said Diane Ablonczy, deputy foreign minister, the day after the coup. This statement was premature. After a confusing initial statement, Lugo rejected his ouster and announced the creation of a parallel government.

A week after the coup the Conservatives participated in an Organization of American States (OAS) mission that many member countries opposed. Largely designed to undermine those countries calling for Paraguay's suspension from the OAS, delegates from the US, Canada, Haiti, Honduras and Mexico traveled to Paraguay to investigate Lugo's removal from office. Ablonczy said the aim of the OAS mission was to "provide important context from Paraguay to inform international reaction. It is important that we avoid a rush to judgment and focus on the best interests of the Paraguayan people." The delegation concluded that the OAS should not suspend Paraguay, which displeased many South American countries.

In an interview three weeks after his ouster Lugo alluded to Ottawa's hostility. "With the current polarization between the United States, Canada and Mexico on one end and South America on the other, we have tried to find regional alternatives. The coup d'etat now attempts to attack the [South American] regional integration efforts." Both the Canadian Labour Congress and the newly formed IndustriALL Global Union criticized the Conservatives' move to recognize the new government.

On a couple of occasions the overthrown president claimed Canadian economic interests contributed to the coup.

"Those who pushed for the coup are those who want to solidify the negotiations with the multinational Rio Tinto Alcan, betraying the energetic sovereignty and interests of our country," Lugo told his supporters one month after the coup. IndustriALL Global Union concurred with the president, sending a letter to the CEO of Rio Tinto. "Rio Tinto, which has a legendary association with the government of Canada, has been quick off the mark to resume negotiations on behalf of Montréal-based Rio Tinto Alcan for a $4 billion aluminum plant," wrote Jyrki Raina, general secretary of IndustriALL Global Union. The labour federation called on "Rio Tinto to publicly disclose its interest and involvement, if any, in the coup d'état in Paraguay and the ousting of a legitimately elected democratic government of Fernando Lugo."

In 2010 Montréal-based Rio Tinto Alcan, a subsidiary of Rio Tinto, began lobbying the Paraguayan government for subsidized electricity to set up a massive aluminum plant near the Paraná River. The company was seeking a 30-year contract that could cost Paraguay's government hundreds of millions of dollars and they received Ottawa's backing. According to international media reports, the Canadian embassy in Buenos Aires, which is in charge of this country's diplomatic relations in Paraguay, lobbied the government on Rio Tinto Alcan's behalf.

The Lugo government was divided over the project, which would consume more energy than the country's entire 6.5 million population and damage the environment. Three weeks before Lugo's ouster Vice-President Federico Franco, who represented an opposition party, complained to *Ultima Hora* newspaper: "I told the President of the Republic (Lugo): why did you send me to Canada to study the [aluminum] project if, finally, a Deputy Minister (Mercedes Canese) was going to oppose it." After the

coup the vice-president became president and Franco announced that negotiations with Rio Tinto Alcan would be fast tracked.

Paraguay was not the first Latin American country where the Conservatives played the role of Ugly Canadians. In 2009 the Harper government tacitly supported the Honduran military's removal of elected president Manuel Zelaya. Early on June 28 soldiers entered the presidential palace and took a pyjama-clad Zelaya to Costa Rica. Soon after demonstrators took to the streets and erected blockades calling for the return of the elected president. In response the military regime imposed marshal law in the capital Tegucigalpa.

Eight hours after Zelaya's ouster a Foreign Affairs spokesperson told Mexico's *Notimex* that Canada had "no comment" regarding the coup. It was not until basically every country in the hemisphere denounced the coup that Ottawa finally did so. *Notimex* later reported that Canada was the only country in the hemisphere that did not explicitly call for Zelaya's return to power and on a number of occasions Peter Kent said it was important to take into account the context in which the military overthrew Zelaya, particularly whether he had violated the constitution. Kent was quoted in the *New York Times* saying: "There is a context in which these events [the coup] happened."

In the lead-up to his ouster the Harper government displayed a clear ambivalence towards Zelaya. With political tensions increasing in Honduras, two days before the coup the Organization of American States (OAS) passed a resolution supporting democracy and the rule of law in that country. Ottawa's representative at the meeting remained silent. Early in June Kent criticized Zelaya, saying: "We have concerns with the government of Honduras." The Conservatives opposed Zelaya's plan for a non-

binding public poll on whether to hold consultations to reopen the constitution, which had been written by a military government. Parroting the baseless accusations of the Honduran oligarchy, Kent said: "There are elections coming up this year and we are watching very carefully the behaviour of the government and what seems to be an attempt to amend the constitution to allow consecutive presidencies."

A week after the coup Zelaya tried to return to Honduras along with three Latin American heads of state. But the military blocked his plane from landing and kept over 100,000 supporters at bay. In doing so the military killed two protesters and wounded at least 30. On CTV Kent blamed Zelaya for the violence.

Just before the elected president tried to fly into Tegucigalpa, Kent told the OAS the "time is not right" for a return, prompting Zelaya to respond dryly: "I could delay until January 27 [2010]" (when his term ended). Two weeks after trying to return by air Zelaya attempted to cross into Honduras by land from Nicaragua. Kent once again criticized this move. "Canada's Kent Says Zelaya Should Wait Before Return to Honduras," read a July 20 Bloomberg news service headline. A July 25 right-wing Honduran newspaper blared: "Canadá pide a Zelaya no entrar al país hasta llegar a un acuerdo" (Canada asks Zelaya not to enter the country until there's a negotiated solution).

Despite the coup Ottawa refused to exclude Honduras from its Military Training Assistance Program. Though only five Honduran troops were being trained in Canada, failing to suspend relations with a military responsible for overthrowing an elected government was highly symbolic. More significantly, Canada was the only major donor to Honduras — the largest recipient of Canadian assistance in Central America — that failed to sever any

aid to the military government. The World Bank, European Union and even the US suspended some of their planned assistance to Honduras.

In response to the conflicting signals from North American leaders, the ousted Honduran foreign minister told *TeleSur* that Ottawa and Washington were providing "oxygen" to the military government. Patricia Rodas called on Canada and the US to suspend aid to the de facto regime. During an official visit to Mexico with Zelaya, Rodas asked Mexican president Felipe Calderon, who was about to meet Harper and Obama, to lobby Ottawa and Washington on their behalf. "We are asking [Calderon] to be an intermediary for our people with the powerful countries of the world, for example, the US and at this moment Canada, which have lines of military and economic support with Honduras."

Five months after Zelaya was ousted the coup government held previously scheduled elections. During the campaign period the de facto government imposed martial law and censored media outlets. Dozens of candidates withdrew from local and national races and opposition presidential candidate Carlos H. Reyes was hospitalized following a severe beating from security forces. A protest in Tegucigalpa on election day was forcefully repressed. Hondurans voted in "a climate of harassment, violence, and violation of the rights to freedom of expression, association and assembly" according to the Washington-based Center for Justice and International Law.

The November 2009 election was boycotted by the UN and OAS and most Hondurans abstained from the poll. Despite mandatory voting regulations, only 45 percent of those eligible cast a ballot (it may have been much lower as this was the government's accounting). Still, Harper's Conservatives endorsed

this electoral farce. "Canada congratulates the Honduran people for the relatively peaceful and orderly manner in which the country's elections were conducted," noted an official statement. Peter Kent went further, boldly proclaiming "there was a strong turnout for the elections, that they appear to have been run freely and fairly, and that there was no major violence."

While most countries in the region continued to shun post-coup Honduras, Ottawa immediately recognized Porfirio Lobo after he was inaugurated as Honduran president on January 27, 2010. Kent stated: "Canada congratulates President Lobo as he begins his term. I am confident that he will provide the strong political leadership needed to help Honduras move beyond its lengthy political impasse." The Conservatives also supported Honduras' re-entry into the OAS, which was opposed by most member states. During a March 2012 visit deputy foreign minister Diane Ablonczy called Honduras an "important" Canadian partner in the Americas.

The coup sparked a major upsurge in grassroots political activism. Hondurans mobilized in support of Zelaya and against the illegitimate government. Protestors also called for more fundamental reforms to their highly unequal society beginning with a constituent assembly to rewrite the country's constitution. The de facto government and elite sectors responded with repression. Amnesty International described "the damage to human rights protection and the rule of law that followed the 2009 coup." In the two years after Zelaya's overthrow hundreds were killed in political violence and many more attacked or injured. A January 2012 *New York Times* op-ed explained: "Impunity reigns. At least 34 members of the opposition have disappeared or been killed, and more than 300 people have been killed by state security forces

since the coup, according to the leading human rights organization Codafeh." That same month a *Miami Herald* editorial pointed out that "Honduras [has] the highest homicide rate in the world. …To make matters worse in Honduras, there are indications that elements of the US-backed government are complicit in the violence and criminality."

Reporters Without Borders noted that at least 19 journalists were killed and none of the murders were solved. In May 2012 the media protection group noted: "His [Erick Avila] death brings to 19 the number of journalists who were supporters of former president Manuel Zelaya, who have been killed since his overthrow in a coup three years ago next month."

The post-coup repression continued, even increased, during Lobo's first two years as president. The Conservatives stayed silent on the detention, torture and murder of anti-coup activists. During an August 2011 visit to Honduras Harper said Canada had "no information to suggest that [human rights abuses] are in any way perpetrated by the government." Deciding this wasn't a sufficient endorsement of the regime's human rights record, the prime minister called Lobo "a prominent human rights leader in this country." According to what criteria? Even if one ignored his role in the state-backed repression, prior to winning a dubious presidential election Lobo attended business school in Miami, oversaw his wealthy family's cattle ranches and was a member of Congress who insisted on reintroducing the death penalty. Few aside from our prime minister would consider that the track record of "a prominent human rights leader."

Just after Harper visited Honduras, noted *Citytv.com*, 150 Canadian soldiers were sent to conduct exercises with that country's military. During Harper's visit the two countries

signed a free trade accord. In the midst of significant state-backed repression the Conservatives gave the regime a boost of legitimacy by commencing bilateral trade negotiations with the Lobo administration in October 2010. Before the coup Ottawa was negotiating a joint trade accord with Honduras, Guatemala, El Salvador and Nicaragua but the Conservatives dropped these plans when they found Lobo more accepting of their conditions.

The Canada-Honduras free trade agreement was largely designed to serve the interests of Canadian investors. Among the biggest players in the small Central American country, Canadian companies had some $600-million invested in Honduras. Ten Honduran human rights organizations responded with a "Pronouncement Rejecting the Extractive Policy of the Government of Canada and the Bilateral Trade Deal between Canada and Honduras." The document claimed the free trade agreement would lead to further abuses by Canadian mining companies.

Just as the interests of investors drove the trade agreement, particular corporate interests motivated Ottawa's hostility towards Zelaya. His move to raise the minimum wage by 60% at the start of 2009 could not have gone down well with one of the world's biggest blank T-shirt makers. At the time of the coup Montréal-based Gildan, which met regularly with Foreign Affairs officials and Canadian politicians, produced about half of its garments in the country. Gildan employed more than 11,000 people in Honduras and the country figured prominently in the company's growth strategy.

Under pressure from the US-based Maquila Solidarity Network, Nike, Gap, and another US-based apparel company operating in Honduras called for the restoration of democracy two weeks after Zelaya was overthrown. Gildan refused to sign this

statement. Without a high-profile brand name Gildan is particularly dependent on producing apparel at the lowest cost possible and was presumably antagonistic towards Zelaya's move to increase the minimum wage.

During his August 2011 trip Harper visited a Gildan facility located in a northern Honduras export processing zone where foreign companies are exempt from taxes as well as standard labour and environmental regulations. "As a general rule, our Canadian companies have a very good record of social responsibility," Harper told reporters on a tour of the facility. "[Gildan] pays above minimum wage. It runs health, nutrition and transport programs for its employees and is a very good corporate citizen."

While the PM sung the company's praise demonstrators carried banners criticizing Gildan's labour practices and Harper's support for the coup. Some Gildan workers tried to deliver an open letter to the prime minister drafted by the Honduran Women's Collective (CODEMUH). It read: "Prime Minister Harper, there have been constant reports of Canadian company Gildan Activewear's anti-organizing and anti-union policies, among other labour violations. For example, Gildan El Progreso in Honduras closed in 2004 to avoid the certification of a union ... Presently, Gildan Activewear is contravening the legal regulations for labour, with regards to treaties and international conventions that protect occupational health and safety, by implementing 4x4 shifts in their factories, where workers work for 4 days straight, 11.5 hours per day, and then have 4 days off. With this system, it's common that on their days off, workers do extra hours, up to 2 day shifts or 2 night shifts. This means that the workweek can be 69 hours long, with a salary of $89.99 (US) per week.

"The production goals or quotas imposed by Gildan Activewear are the highest in the industry in Honduras. To earn $89.99 per week, workers have to produce 550 dozen pieces every day, and are exposed to awkward postures, executing up to 40,000 repetitive movements in their joints, tendons, and muscles per day. These conditions produce Occupational Musculoskeletal Injuries (MSI) ... In Honduras, Gildan does not pay taxes because they are exempt."

The mining sector was another beneficiary of the trade accord and other post-coup political changes. In 2008 Zelaya responded to grassroots pressure and announced that no new mining concessions would be granted, much to the chagrin of the Canadian mining companies that dominated Honduras' extractive industry. The coup interrupted the final reading of a proposed mining law that called for greater community consent for mining projects as well as an end to open-pit mining and the use of cyanide in new concessions. It also raised royalty rates.

Rights Action uncovered credible information that a subsidiary of Vancouver-based Goldcorp, the world's second biggest gold producer, provided money to those who rallied in support of the coup. "On a number of occasions, mine workers, ex-mine workers and other local young men, have travelled in buses from the Siria Valley to Tegucigalpa to participate in pro-coup marches organized by the pro-coup Movement for Peace and Democracy that is funded by the Honduran private sector. ... The buses from the Siria Valley are contracted to Entremares [Goldcorp's wholly owned subsidiary]; These bus trips are coordinated by local men who work or used to work with Entremares; who work or used to work as 'community promoters' with the Fundacion San Martin (a local NGO set up and funded

by Entremares); and who work with the Honduran Association of Mining, that Entremares is a member of … The men and young men are contacted one by one, and asked if they would like to go on the bus, for 400 Lempiras (over US$20). If they agree, they are told to meet at such and such a point, in the Siria Valley, and the bus picks them up in the morning … When the bus gets to the protest, in Tegucigalpa, they are wearing their white t-shirts [the colour of the coup supporters]. They are told to stay in the area of the protest, and to meet back at the bus at 3 pm. They were told to shout along with the pro-democracy and pro-peace slogans of the pro-coup rally organizers."

Soon after Lobo took office, Canadian government and mining officials began pressing the president to pass a new mining law. The English language *Honduras Weekly* reported on a February 2010 meeting: "President Porfirio Lobo met Tuesday with Canada's ambassador to Honduras, Neil Reeder, and a group of Canadian businessmen, including the president of Aura Minerals, Inc., Patrick Downey, and investor David Petroff. … Ambassador Reeder expressed his interest in expanding Canada's investments in the Honduran mining and maquila sectors. He specifically mentioned the need to establish new mining regulations that would both protect the interests of foreign mining companies in Honduras and create transparency in mining operations. Mr. Reeder estimated potential investments in Honduras of up to US$700 million and pointed out the benefits to the country in terms of jobs creation and additional tax revenues. Mining in Honduras by foreign multinationals has traditionally been a source of contention, with one side arguing in favour of business interests and another pointing out the environmental damages caused by open pit mining and the use of chemicals such as cyanide."

At the 2012 Prospectors and Developers Association of Canada convention International Trade Minister Ed Fast met Honduras' Natural Resources Minister Rigoberto Cuellar and the head of the Directorate for the Promotion of Mining Aldo Santos. In describing the two Honduran officials' visit to Canada a Foreign Affairs document, uncovered by Mining Watch's Jennifer Moore, explained: "Honduras is in the process of transformation from the anti-mining Zelaya administration to the pro-sustainable mining and pro-CSR Lobo government." In April 2012 the mining watchdog also reported that the embassy in Honduras sponsored a workshop on "corporate social responsibility" at which the Canadian ambassador claimed this country works to ensure "benefits for communities where mines operate." Canadian government and industry lobbying led Honduran legislators to hire experts from this country – reportedly paid by Ottawa – for advice on writing their mining laws.

After visiting Honduras, Nobel Peace Prize winner Jody Williams wrote in the *Ottawa Citizen* about the country's planned mining legislation. The "proposed law would accelerate the licensing process for new mines in Honduras, including open-pit mines, and simplify the rules for mining companies planning to operate in Honduras. It would also reduce environmental standards and privilege water use by mining companies. At the same time, the new law would open the door for foreign states to become title owners of mining concessions, and it fails to ensure the communities that will suffer the most direct impact from the mining have any meaningful say over mining."

Besides particular corporate interests, Harper supported the coup in Honduras in order to block the progressive social transformation taking place across Latin America. The

Conservatives opposed Zelaya because his government was moving closer to the governments in the region leading the push towards a more united Latin America. A year before Zelaya was overthrown Honduras joined the Bolivarian Alliance for the People of Our Americas (ALBA), which is a response to North American capitalist domination of the region. Led by Venezuela, ALBA is "an international cooperation organization based on the idea of social, political, and economic integration" among Latin American and Caribbean countries. Post-coup Honduras withdrew from the alliance.

Threatened by Venezuela's attempts to move away from capitalism and Washington-led diplomacy, the Conservatives supported the US campaign to undermine and replace that country's elected government. When Hugo Chavez was re-elected president with 63 percent of the vote in December 2006, 32 members of the OAS supported a resolution to congratulate him for winning an election monitored by the organization. Canada was the only member to join the US in opposing a message of congratulations.

Just after Chavez's re-election US assistant secretary of state for hemispheric affairs, Thomas Shannon, called Canada "a country that can deliver messages that can resonate in ways that sometimes our messages don't for historical or psychological reasons." Six months later Harper toured South America to help stunt the region's rejection of neoliberalism and US dependence. ("To show [the region] that Canada functions and that it can be a better model than Venezuela," in the words of a high-level Foreign Affairs official quoted by *Le Devoir*.) During the trip, Harper and his entourage made a number of comments critical of the Chavez government. Since that time the prime minister has continued to demonize a government that massively expanded the

population's access to health and education services. In April 2009 Harper responded to a question regarding Venezuela by saying: "I don't take any of these rogue states lightly." A month earlier, the prime minister referred to the far right Colombian government as a valuable "ally" in a hemisphere full of "serious enemies and opponents."

The Conservatives levelled all manner of baseless accusations against the Venezuelan government. In September 2010, minister Kent said: "This is an election month in Venezuela and the official media has again fired up some of the anti-Semitic slurs against the Jewish community as happened during the Gaza incursion." Virginie Levesque, a spokesperson for the Canadian Embassy in Venezuela, also accused the Chavez government of racism against Jews. "The Canadian Embassy has encouraged and continues to encourage the Venezuelan government to follow through on its commitment to reject and combat anti-Semitism and to do its utmost to ensure the security of the Jewish community and its religious and cultural centers." Even the head of Canada's military joined the onslaught of condemnation against Venezuela. After a tour of South America in early 2010, Walter Natynczyk wrote: "Regrettably, some countries, such as Venezuela, are experiencing the politicization of their armed forces." (A Canadian general criticizing another country's military is, of course, not political.)

When the Conservatives prorogued parliament to avoid further debate about prisoner abuse in Afghanistan, Kent visited Venezuela. After meeting opposition figures in January 2010 the deputy foreign minister told the media: "Democratic space within Venezuela has been shrinking and in this election year, Canada is very concerned about the rights of all Venezuelans to participate in

the democratic process." Kent continued: "During my recent visit to Venezuela, I heard many individuals and organizations express concerns related to violations of the right to freedom of expression and other basic liberties." Venezuela's Ambassador to the OAS Roy Chaderton Matos responded by saying the Conservatives support "coup plotters" and "destabilizers" in Venezuela. "I am talking of a Canada governed by an ultra right that closed its Parliament for various months to (evade) an investigation over the violation of human rights — I am talking about torture and assassinations — by its soldiers in Afghanistan."

The Harper government's attacks against Venezuela were part of a campaign to support Latin America's US-backed business class. According to a cable Wikileaks released, the US embassy in Ottawa pushed Canada to begin "engaging more actively in other hemispheric trouble spots such as Venezuela, Colombia, and Cuba." In July 2007 the Conservatives announced an Americas strategy as part of a bid to win "outsize[d] influence" in Washington. The Spring 2011 *International Journal* noted: "Although Canada has not openly named its partners in the region within the new America's strategy, these may easily be discerned from the countries that the Prime Minister and former Governor General Michaelle Jean visited in the past few years, namely Mexico, Colombia, Chile, Peru, Haiti and the Caribbean in general." Absent from this list were more left-leaning governments in Venezuela, Nicaragua, Ecuador, Paraguay, Argentina, Uruguay and Bolivia.

In March 2010 trade minister Van Loan admitted that the "secondary" goal of Canada's free trade agreement with Colombia was to bolster that country's right wing government against its Venezuelan neighbour. The *Globe and Mail* explained: "The

Canadian government's desire to bolster fledgling free-market democracies in Latin America in an ideological competition with left-leaning, authoritarian nationalists like Venezuela's Hugo Chavez is rarely expressed with force, even though it is at the heart of an Ottawa initiative." An unnamed Conservative told the paper: "For countries like Peru and Colombia that are trying be helpful in the region, I think everybody's trying to keep them attached to the free-market side of the debate in Latin America, rather than sloshing them over into the Bolivarian [Venezuelan] side."

Harper devoted a great deal of energy to backing the most repressive and right wing government in Latin America. According to an April 2009 cable from the US embassy in Ottawa, in private the PM conceded that the Colombia trade accord was unpopular with Canadians. Released by Wikileaks the cable noted: "It was a painful but deliberate choice for the Prime Minister" to support president Alvaro Uribe in the face of stiff resistance to the free trade agreement, particularly from Canada's labour movement.

The Conservatives shifted aid to the Western hemisphere from Africa largely to stunt Latin America's growing rejection of neoliberal capitalism and US dependence. The aim was to strengthen the region's right-wing governments and civil society organizations. Only a limited amount of Canadian aid in the Americas supported the governments and civil society groups leading the charge against neoliberalism and US domination. Rather, the majority of aid money flowed to those whose views most closely aligned with the Conservatives.

To combat independent-minded, socialist-oriented governments and movements the Conservatives "played a more active role in supporting US ideologically-driven [democracy promotion] initiatives," noted researcher Neil A. Burron. Writing

in the Spring 2011 *International Journal* he further explained: "Canadian democracy promotion is increasingly being used as a political device to promote free markets and to criticize governments that have strayed from the Washington [free-market capitalist] consensus." In 2009 the Conservatives opened a South America-focused "democracy promotion" centre at the Canadian Embassy in Peru. Staffed by two diplomats, this secretive venture may clash with the OAS' non-intervention clause. "One foreign affairs official who was interviewed [by Burron] stated that the department is increasingly focusing on representative democracy as defined by the OAS Inter-American Democratic charter. She noted that even the emphasis on 'citizens' in the new program had been controversial since it could be used to defend notions of 'popular democracy' advanced by populist regimes such as the one in Venezuela."

According to documents unearthed by journalist Anthony Fenton, in November 2007 Ottawa gave the Justice and Development Consortium (Asociación Civil Consorcio Desarrollo y Justicia) $94,580 "to consolidate and expand the democracy network in Latin America and the Caribbean." Also funded by the Washington-based National Endowment for Democracy (NED — a quasi CIA front group) the Justice and Development Consortium worked to unite opposition to leftist Latin American governments. Similarly, in the spring of 2008 the Canadian embassy in Panama teamed up with the NED to organize a meeting for prominent members of the opposition in Venezuela, Bolivia, Cuba and Ecuador. It was designed to respond to the "new era of populism and authoritarianism in Latin America." The meeting spawned the Red Latinoamericana y del Caribe para la Democracia, "which brings together mainstream NGOs critical of the leftist governments in the hemisphere."

Washington spent tens of millions of dollars funding groups opposed to the Venezuelan government. The foremost researcher on US funding to the anti-Chavez opposition, Eva Golinger, claimed Canadian groups were also involved, and according to a May 2010 report from Spanish NGO Fride, "Canada is the third most important provider of democracy assistance" to Venezuela after the US and Spain. Burron describes an interview with a Canadian "official [who] repeatedly expressed concerns about the quality of democracy in Venezuela, noting that the [Federal government's] Glyn Berry program provided funds to a 'get out the vote' campaign in the last round of elections in that country." You can bet it wasn't designed to get Chavez supporters to the polls.

The Conservatives are not forthcoming with information about the groups they fund in Venezuela. Since 2005, notes *Imperialist Canada*, CIDA has refused to release the names of groups they fund in Venezuela because they claim this would endanger those organizations. We know, however, that the Canadian government's "arms-length" human rights organization, Rights & Democracy (R&D) gave its 2010 John Humphrey Award to Venezuelan NGO PROVEA (El Programa Venezolano de Educacion-Accion en Derechos Humanos). The award included a $30,000 grant and a "speaking tour of Canadian cities to help increase awareness of the recipient's human rights work." PROVEA was highly critical of Venezuela's elected government. In December 2008 Venezuela's interior and justice minister called PROVEA "liars" who were "paid in [US] dollars." During a September 2010 visit "to meet with representatives of PROVEA and other [Venezuelan] organizations devoted to human rights and democratic development" the Conservatives' highly controversial

appointee as President of R&D, Gérard Latulippe, blogged about his and PROVEA's political views. "Marino [Betancourt, Director General of PROVEA] told me about recent practices of harassment and criminalization of the government towards civil society organizations." In another post Latulippe explained: "We have witnessed in recent years the restriction of the right to freedom of expression. Since 2004-2005, the government of President Chavez has taken important legislative measures which limit this right." Upon returning to Canada, Latulippe cited Venezuela as a country with "no democracy". He told *Embassy*: "You can see the emergence of a new model of democracy, where in fact it's trying to make an alternative to democracy by saying people can have a better life even if there's no democracy. You have the example of Russia. You have an example of Venezuela."

Latulippe's claims have no basis in reality. On top of improving living conditions for the country's poor, the Chavez-led government/movement massively increased democratic space through community councils, new political parties, grassroots media and worker cooperatives. More than any other political party in the hemisphere, they also won a dozen elections/referendums since 1998 (and lost only one).

Funded almost entirely by the federal government, R&D took its cues from Foreign Affairs and the simple truth is that the Harper government supports the old Latin American business interests that have long worked with the US empire. They did so even when this cost Canada's standing in the region. An internal Spring 2011 evaluation of the Americas Strategy by Foreign Affairs' office of the inspector general concluded: "There is evidence to suggest Canada's credibility in the region could decline." Beginning in December 2009 all the Latin American and Caribbean nations

convened a series of summits to discuss regional economic and political integration. Unlike meetings of the Organization of American States, Cuba was invited to this summit. But, the US and Canada were not. A memo released by Wikileaks explained the regional sentiment: "The Latinos don't want the US at the table and they see Canada as an extension of the US." When the Community of Latin American and Caribbean States was formed in February 2010 Canada and the US were excluded. A message about Canada's standing in the region was sent.

Neoliberalism

Harper has firmly and consistently supported Canada's banks, which are some of the largest financial institutions in the world. In fact, the Conservatives repeatedly defended the interests of international financiers over ordinary Canadians or even small investors.

As a means to regulate speculation in financial markets, in November 2009 UK prime minister Gordon Brown proposed a tiny (ranging from .005% to 1%) tax on international financial transactions. Worried about the plight of investment bankers Canadian Finance Minister Jim Flaherty immediately dismissed the idea of a global 'Tobin Tax'. "That's not something that we would want to do. We're not in the business of raising taxes," said Flaherty. For his part, Harper admitted to blocking the G20's bid for an international banking tax. The prime minister told the July 2011 issue of *Maclean's*: "Whether it's taking strong and clear positions, for instance, at the G20 on something like a global financial regulation and a banking tax, we don't just say, 'Well, a consensus is developing for that. We'll go along with it.' It was not in our interest. It actually happens to be bad policy as well."

The Conservatives even opposed Washington's late 2011 move to restrict some of the high risk/high return banking activities that led to the 2008 economic collapse (the so-called "Volcker rule"). Flaherty and Bank of Canada governor Mark Carney both sent letters to US decision-makers criticizing the reforms. "I am writing to express my concerns regarding the proposed Volcker rule, which could have material adverse effects on Canadian financial institutions and markets," wrote Flaherty in February 2012. Flaherty and Carney intervened following a bid by US bankers to spark international opposition to the reforms. That combined with Canadian banks owning major assets in the US helps explain the Conservatives' position.

The Conservatives' unyielding support for bankers and big investors shaped their response to the European economic crisis. Harper backed Germany's push for other European governments to cut social spending in the face of an economic downturn. During a June 2011 visit to Athens Harper forcefully backed austerity measures bitterly resisted by much of the Greek population. "I certainly admire the determination of Prime Minister Papandreou, and the very difficult actions he's had to undertake in response to problems his government did not create. So we are very much all on his side."

When German Chancellor Angela Merkel visited Ottawa in August 2012 Harper reiterated his support for austerity measures. He said "there are additional things that have to be done" by European governments to end the continent's economic troubles. "One of the things I appreciate about Chancellor Merkel's leadership is the willingness, including at times of urgency and stress, to not just find any solution but to find correct and good solutions," Harper added.

Canada joined the US in opposing the International Monetary Fund's bid to raise $400-billion to build a financial buffer against the Eurozone debt crisis. This put Ottawa at odds with almost the entire G20. A June 2012 *Maclean's* article explained: "When Thomas Mulcair voiced support for the IMF plan the Conservative attack machine suddenly revved up, and a succession of Tory MPs took turns denouncing the NDP leader for asking 'Canadians to tighten their belts so they can hand out billions of dollars to Europe,' in the process putting 'a huge burden on the economy here.'" This was nonsense, noted Scott Clark, former Canadian deputy finance minister and chief representative to the IMF. "Funds are not given to the IMF; funds are lent to the IMF. More importantly the funds that would be lent to the IMF would not come from Canadian taxpayers. The funds would come from foreign exchange reserves held at the Bank of Canada. As of May 23, 2012 Canada had foreign exchange reserves of $68.7 billion. ... Were Canada to contribute to the G-20 fund the 'contribution' would involve a transfer of SDRs [special drawing rights] from the exchange reserves to the IMF in exchange for a commitment that the funds would be repaid. There would be no use of taxpayers' money and there would be no budgetary impact." But, why let the facts get in the way of a political attack.

Rotterdam Convention

The final example of Harper's over-the-top, pro-capitalist, policy is one of the grossest elements of Canadian foreign policy.

On a number of occasions the Conservatives blocked consensus at the Rotterdam Convention to place chrysotile asbestos, a known carcinogen, on its list of dangerous products. Despite Canadian and international research highlighting the risks

from asbestos exposure, in October 2006 Canada successfully convinced the Rotterdam Convention to postpone a decision to place chrysotile asbestos on its list of dangerous products. Even after widespread campaigning about the hazards of the product in the lead-up to the next two Convention meetings, the Conservatives still opposed adding asbestos to its list of dangerous products.

In a rare political statement, "Canada's doctors blast Harper government's asbestos policy", noted a *Vancouver Sun* headline. Ninety-nine percent of delegates to the Canadian Medical Association's August 2011 general assembly voted to criticize the government's "shameful" decision to block listing asbestos as a hazardous product. In private, Health Canada told the government to back the listing as did 200 environmental, health and labour groups that signed an open letter calling on Harper to stop preventing the Rotterdam Convention from adding chrysotile asbestos to its list of hazardous substances. Instead, the Conservatives directly supported the domestic asbestos industry. They gave the Chrysotile Institute lobby group \$250,000 a year and in October 2010 an aide to natural resources minister Christian Paradis resigned after he was caught meddling in access-to-information requests relating to "the backgrounds of members of a government panel examining asbestos." Paradis' riding is home to Canada's last remaining asbestos mine, which singlehandedly makes this country one of the largest exporters of this carcinogen.

As part of negotiations for an economic agreement the Conservatives worked to eliminate a 10 percent duty on Canadian asbestos exports. A December 2011 *Asian Journal* headline reacting to this news dubbed it "Harper's Christmas Gift to Poor Indians".

Tens of thousands of Indians have begun to die from asbestos exposure.

10. Questionable Judgement

While Harper's foreign policy has largely been driven by narrow political and economic interests, sometimes in their eagerness to emulate and follow US neoconservatives they've displayed tragic incompetence or confusion. Canada's role in Somalia and Haiti are good examples of the tragic, while Conservative foreign policy towards the most populous country in the world has been contradictory and confusing.

Somalia

After the failed US invasion of Somalia in the early 1990s (Black Hawk Down) American forces once again attacked that country in December 2006. After the Islamic Courts Union won control of Mogadishu and the south of the country from an assortment of warlords, American forces launched air attacks and 50,000 Ethiopian troops invaded Somalia. According to a cable released by Wikileaks, the US under secretary of state for Africa, Jendayi Frazer, pressed Ethiopia's Prime Minister Meles Zenawi to intervene. The Conservatives supported this aggression in which as many as 20,000 Somalis were killed and hundreds of thousands displaced. Throughout 2007 and 2008 when the US launched periodic airstrikes and Ethiopian troops occupied Somalia, Ottawa added its military presence. At various points during 2008, *HMCS Calgary*, *HMCS Iroquois, HMCS Charlottetown*, *HMCS Protecteur*, *HMCS Toronto* and *HMCS Ville de Québec* all patrolled off the coast of Somalia. In the summer of 2008 Canada took command of NATO's Task Force 150 that worked off the coast of Somalia.

The Conservatives' public comments on Somalia broadly supported Ethiopian/US actions. They made no criticism of the US bombings and when prominent Somali-Canadian journalist Ali Iman Sharmarke was assassinated in Mogadishu in August 2007 foreign minister Mackay only condemned "the violence" in the country. He never mentioned that the assassins were pro-government militia members with ties to Ethiopian troops.

The Conservatives backed a February 2007 UN Security Council resolution that called for an international force in Somalia. "Canada welcomes the United Nations Security Council's unanimous adoption this week of Resolution 1744, which authorizes the deployment of an African Union peace stabilization force." The Conservatives also endorsed the Ethiopia-installed Somali government, which had operated in exile. A February 2007 Foreign Affairs release noted: "We welcome Somali President Abdullahi Yusuf Ahmed's announcement to urgently convene a national reconciliation congress involving all stakeholders, including political, clan and religious leaders, and representatives of civil society." In April 2009 the Somali transitional government's minister of diaspora affairs and ambassador to Kenya were feted in Ottawa. Supported by outsiders, the transitional government had little backing among Somalis. An Oxfam report explained: "The TFG [transitional federal government] is not accepted as legitimate by much of the population. Unelected and widely perceived as externally imposed through a process that sidelined sub-national authorities and wider civil society, the transitional federal institutions face strong allegations of corruption and aid diversion."

In maybe the strongest signal of Canadian support for the outside intervention, Ottawa did not make its aid to Ethiopia contingent on its withdrawal from Somalia. Instead they increased

assistance to this strategic ally. Among CIDA's largest recipients, Ethiopia received about $150 million annually in Canadian aid from 2008 to 2011.

Aid to Ethiopia was controversial and not only because that country invaded and occupied its neighbour. An October 2010 *Globe and Mail* headline noted: "Ethiopia using Canadian aid as a political weapon, rights group says." Human Rights Watch researcher Felix Horne claimed Ottawa contravened its own Official Development Assistance Accountability Act by continuing to pump aid into Ethiopia despite its failure to meet international human-rights standards. In addition to arbitrary detentions, widespread torture and attacks on political opponents, the Ethiopian government systematically forced rural villagers off their land.

Canadian aid to Ethiopia faced another challenge. In February 2012 the family of a Somali Canadian businessman sued the Conservatives to get them to stop sending aid to Ethiopia until Bashir Makhtal was released from prison. In January 2007 Makhtal was "rendered" illegally from Kenya to Ethiopia, imprisoned without access to a lawyer or consular official for 18 months and then given a life sentence. The lawsuit was a last ditch effort by the Makhtal family to force the Harper government's hand. Amnesty had already taken up Makhtal's cause declaring that "Prime Minister Harper must intervene to assist Canadian citizen Bashir Makhtal imprisoned in Ethiopia." But the efforts were to no avail. While John Baird, who has many Somali Canadians in his Ottawa riding, made a number of public comments in support of Makhtal, the Conservatives failed to seriously push Ethiopia on his release. When Ethiopian Prime Minster Meles Zenawi was invited to the 2010 G20 Summit in Toronto, for instance, the

Conservatives failed to raise Makhtal's case. The NDP claimed the government was indifferent to the plight of non-white Canadians imprisoned in foreign countries. While this may partly explain the Conservatives' indifference towards Makhtal's plight they were also wary of conflict with Ethiopia, a strategic Western ally on the border of Sudan and Somalia. For the Ethiopian government, imprisoning Makhtal was a way to deliver a message to its opponents because Makhtal's grandfather was a founder of the Ogaden National Liberation Front, a rebel group that continues to fight for the independence of the southeastern portion of the Somali Regional State that is currently part of Ethiopia. For the paranoid Ethiopian state the fact Makhtal left Somalia when the Islamic Courts Union collapsed proved that he collaborated with the "terrorist" Al Shabaab.

In early 2009 Ethiopian troops withdrew from Somalia (they reinvaded in late 2011 and continued to occupy parts of the country as this book went to print). The Conservatives helped finance the African Union force that replaced the Ethiopian troops. At the end of 2011 Canada gave $1 million to the UN Trust Fund for the African Union Mission in Somalia (AMISOM). Ottawa also paid to deploy a police unit from Uganda to Somalia while the US paid, trained and armed most of the force. In July 2012 the *Los Angeles Times* reported: "The U.S. has been quietly equipping and training thousands of African soldiers to wage a widening proxy war against the Shabaab. ... Officially, the troops are under the auspices of the African Union. But in truth ... the 15,000-strong force pulled from five African countries is largely a creation of the State Department and Pentagon, trained and supplied by the U.S. government and guided by dozens of retired foreign military personnel hired through private contractors."

Ottawa strongly supported the US-backed African Union force. An August 2010 Foreign Affairs release explained: "Canada supports the mandate of the African Union Mission in Somalia." Baird also praised the February 2012 UN Security Council vote to increase the number of international troops in Somalia by almost 50 percent to nearly 18,000. The foreign minister said: "Canada is encouraged by recent gains made by troops from Somalia and other African nations, who have pushed Al Shabaab out of Mogadishu and other areas in south-central Somalia."

The Conservatives repeatedly verbally attacked Al Shabaab, which had been the youth wing of the Islamic Courts Union before the Ethiopian/US invasion. The group waged a violent campaign against the foreign forces in the country and Somalia's transitional government. "Canada wants to condemn in the strongest terms the actions of the terrorist group Al Shabaab", noted Baird in February 2012. Following Washington's lead, the Conservatives added Al Shabaab to Canada's terrorist list in March 2010.

Ottawa also made it illegal for Canadians to provide financial assistance to the Eritrean military because that country was accused of supplying and training Al Shabaab. "Canada is concerned by Eritrea's support of armed opposition groups in Somalia," said Dana Cryderman, a Foreign Affairs spokeswoman. Canadian banks were also ordered to freeze the assets of Eritrean political leaders and military officials and Ottawa banned weapons sales to the small East African country that has spent most of the past 50 years at war with its much larger neighbour Ethiopia.

Canada's support for foreign intervention in Somalia did not go unnoticed. When a group calling themselves Mujahedin of Somalia abducted a Canadian and Australian in October 2008 they

accused Canada and Australia of "taking part in the destruction of Somalia." They demanded a change in policy from these two countries. Similarly, in October 2011 an Al Shabaab official cited Canada as one of a handful of countries that deserved to be attacked.

Portrayed by Washington and Ottawa as simply a struggle against Islamic terrorism, the intervention in Somalia was driven by geopolitical and economic considerations. A significant amount of the world's goods, notably oil from the Persian Gulf, pass near the country's 1,000-mile coastline and whoever controls this territory is well placed to exert influence over this shipping.

There are also oil deposits in the country. A February 2012 *Observer* headline noted: "Why defeat of Al Shabaab could mean an oil bonanza for western firms in Somalia." With plans to invest more than $50 million, Vancouver-based Africa Oil began drilling an exploratory well in northern Somalia's semi-autonomous Puntland region at the start of 2012. This was the first significant oil drilling in Somalia in two decades. The Canadian company didn't escape the eye of Al Shabaab. A Twitter post from the group's press office called Africa Oil's contracts "non-binding". "Western companies must be fully aware that all exploration rights and drilling contracts in N. Eastern Somalia are now permanently nullified", the group's spokesperson wrote. In an interview with *Maclean's* Africa Oil CEO Keith Hill acknowledged the "significant" security risks and costs for their operations in Somalia but he noted the rarity of a "billion-barrel oil field".

China

When the Conservatives took power in 2006 they said they would change Canadian policy towards China. Previous

governments, according to the ardently pro-business Harper, prioritized Canadian business interests, turning a blind eye to Chinese human rights violations. Harper was quoted by the *Globe and Mail* in November 2006 as saying he wouldn't "sell out" on human rights with China. But one day earlier natural resources minister Gary Lunn was quoted in the business pages of the same paper saying: "I would like to encourage Chinese investment in Canada. Partnering with Canadian companies can help you secure the minerals and metals that China needs to fulfill its economic development. … we invite Chinese mining companies to jointly explore and develop these and other deposits in Canada."

To help investors, in June 2008, the Conservatives announced they were opening six new trade offices in cities across China. The government saw no problem with Pratt and Whitney selling Canadian-built engines for China's newest attack helicopter. Nor did they stop Nortel from selling its highly advanced OPTera surveillance technology to China's security forces. Nortel also provided equipment used in China's surveillance architecture in Tibet, technology, that some said, would lead to the permanent militarization of the Tibetan plateau. The Conservatives were happy to meet with the Dalai Lama but did nothing to stop Canadian companies from assisting China's further colonization of Tibet. Bombardier provided the Chinese with trains for its state of the art railway to Tibet and a number of Canadian mining companies (Continental Minerals, Hunter- Dixon and Inter-Citic Minerals) operated in the region. Harper's criticism of China was designed to appeal to Canadians who supported a human rights oriented foreign policy, but also to please the hawks in Washington.

Harper's anti-Chinese comments reflected a worldview that longs for a divided and imperially dominated country like pre-

1949 China. A weak China would increase the West's power and in the long term would likely benefit foreign investors. But in the short term there was a fundamental tension between the right wing geopolitical position, represented in Harper's criticism of China, and Canadian corporate interests. China was a large market and a great place to invest, which is why Nancy Hughes Anthony, president of the Canadian Bankers' Association, responded to Harper's comments by saying: "We are not the body that is going to judge China on the basis of any of its human rights record, and they may have comments for us on things that are happening in our domestic area." Montréal's *La Presse*, which is owned by the founder of the Canada-China Business Council, Paul Desmarais, was also highly critical of Harper's attacks against China.

After the push back from Desmarais and some other leading capitalists the Conservatives toned down their criticism of China. But, as Washington's focus turned to countering that country's power in Asia Ottawa ramped up its belligerence. In June 2012 the Canadian Press reported: "Canada is seeking a deal with Singapore to establish a military staging post there as part of its effort to support the United States' 'pivot' toward Asia to counter a rising China." The news agency quoted Peter MacKay at the Shangri-La Dialogue saying "this entire concept — the buzzword is the pivot to the Pacific — it's a recognition of the regional power dynamics here that do affect us with China expanding and modernizing their military capabilities."

In 2011 Washington increased its military presence around China. *Antiwar.com* explains: "The so-called 'Asia pivot' is an aggressive policy that involves surging American military presence throughout the region – in the Philippines, Japan, Australia, Guam, South Korea, Singapore, etc. – in an unprovoked

scheme to contain rising Chinese economic and military influence." Concurrently, Washington stoked tension between China and its neighbours over territorial disputes in the potentially resource-rich South China Sea. The US effectively told the Philippines, Vietnam, Taiwan, Malaysia and Brunei that they would back them in their longstanding territorial disputes with China.

During his June 2012 trip to the Shangri-La Dialogue in Singapore MacKay publicly parroted the US position that China is a threat. He referred to China as "the 500-pound gorilla" and claimed countries in the region were worried about its power. "In the hallways here what I'm hearing is there's a lot of tension, it's [China] seen as provocative by countries here," said MacKay.

During the Shangri-La Dialogue it was announced that 1,400 Canadian Forces' personnel would participate in the summer 2012 Rim of the Pacific military exercise. The military spent heavily to send five ships, a submarine, 15 planes, helicopters, dive teams, and 150 infantry to this US-led Asian military exercise that does not include China.

But business ties pull Canada closer to China. Which pull will be the strongest for the Conservatives? Profitable business deals? Or right wing geopolitical concerns? Right now confusion reigns.

Militarizing post-earthquake Haiti

After a deadly earthquake rocked Haiti on January 12, 2010, most Canadians worried about uncovering those trapped, getting water to survivors and connecting family members. But, it seems the Harper government was concerned about something very different. According to internal documents the Canadian Press examined a year after the disaster, officials in Ottawa feared a post-

earthquake power vacuum could lead to a "popular uprising". One briefing note marked "secret" explained: "Political fragility has increased the risks of a popular uprising, and has fed the rumour that ex-president Jean-Bertrand Aristide, currently in exile in South Africa, wants to organize a return to power." The documents also explained the importance of strengthening the Haitian authorities' ability "to contain the risks of a popular uprising."

To police Haiti's traumatized and suffering population 2,050 Canadian troops were deployed alongside 12,000 US soldiers and 1,500 UN troops (8,000 UN soldiers were already there). Even though there was no war, for a period there were more foreign troops in Haiti per square kilometer than in Afghanistan or Iraq (and about as many per capita).

Though the Conservatives rapidly deployed 2,050 troops they ignored calls to dispatch this country's Heavy Urban Search and Rescue (HUSAR) Teams, which are trained to "locate trapped persons in collapsed structures". "The government had opted to send Canadian Armed Forces instead," the *Toronto Sun* reported. "While the humanitarian crisis rages in Haiti, Toronto's highly-skilled emergency response team is stuck on Bermondsey Rd. in a mock training session. Instead of being on the ground in earthquake-ravaged Port-au-Prince — doing what it is they are trained to do and eager to do — the modern-equipped, taxpayer-funded Heavy Urban Search and Rescue (HUSAR) team is on the sidelines while people suffer."

When pressed to explain why the government sent soldiers instead of the HUSAR Teams in Toronto, Calgary, Halifax, Winnipeg, Montréal and Vancouver, foreign minister Cannon resorted to deception. He told the *Toronto Sun*: "When you deploy Canadian armed forces, they can hit the ground and

they are literally capable of sustaining themselves, not only through food necessity but they do have the equipment required to camp there, to set up there. My understanding is that these capabilities aren't necessarily there for the group [HUSAR] that you are referring too." In another interview Cannon was more direct, claiming: "They [HUSAR] don't have the expertise nor the equipment to do what's needed in Haiti." Not true. Capable of dispatching in six hours, HUSAR teams can sustain themselves for ten days without re-supplying and they possess food, water and medical equipment/services to distribute. A number of other countries such as Iceland and China sent their search and rescue teams. The Conservatives simply prioritized the military in the face of the incredible suffering caused by Haiti's earthquake. As a result of decisions made in Ottawa and Washington some poor neighbourhoods in Port-au-Prince received no outside search and rescue help. Survivors were left to dig family and friends out of collapsed buildings on their own.

Though they were largely focused on 'security', the Conservatives knew the public wanted Canada to aid earthquake victims. As such, they claimed Canadian troops were deployed to alleviate Haitian suffering. Harper told the press: "Ships of the Atlantic fleet were immediately ordered to Haiti from Halifax, loaded with relief supplies." Not true. "A [Halifax] *Chronicle Herald* reporter and photographer embedded with the military for the mission observed that they didn't have much food, water, medical equipment or tents to distribute, beyond what they needed for their own crews." Nor did the other Canadian naval vessel dispatched have supplies to distribute. The Canadian Press reported: "*HMCS Athabaskan* brings little in terms of actual food and water, but is more equipped to provide support to existing

agencies, to provide leadership in chaotic communities and to better assess their needs and priorities."

In the face of widespread public empathy the Conservatives were sensitive about their image after the earthquake. A *Toronto Star* access to information request found that two weeks after the quake the government diverted a flight carrying orphans from Montréal to Ottawa for a photo opportunity. "Haitian orphans destined for Québec, many of them cold and exhausted, were rerouted through Ottawa for what critics say was nothing more than a photo-op for the Harper government." Widely criticized for failing to fast-track adoptions already in process, immigration minister Jason Kenney met the kids at the airport.

Further proof that the government was more concerned with controlling Haiti than aiding earthquake victims came when Canadian troops withdrew. Seven weeks after its arrival the Canadian military abruptly departed Jacmel. Aid groups pleaded with the Canadian Forces to leave the heavy lift equipment they brought to unload cargo ships at the port and the portable communications equipment they used to open the city's airport, but the military ignored the requests. As a result, the airport was closed to international traffic and the flow of aid through the seaport was slowed. Two weeks after Canadian troops left Jacmel the *Globe and Mail* described a "vacuum that seems to be sucking parts of the city they [Canadian troops] worked so hard to rebuild not forwards but back." A US aid worker told the paper: "I love team Canada ... But you came to stabilize and you created more destabilization by taking things away."

When the media was focused on Haiti the Canadian Forces used their considerable capacities to take charge of the airport and seaport. But, after the media gaze dissipated and the

political situation stabilized Ottawa called the troops home. In so doing the Canadian Forces ignored the responsibility that ought to have accompanied the power they amassed in Jacmel. It may be that, despite the efforts of the individual soldiers, the Canadian Forces left Jacmel worse off in the long run. It was certainly more difficult for the airport and seaport to secure the equipment required two months after the quake when international attention had dissipated.

The files uncovered by the Canadian Press about the government's post-earthquake concerns go to the heart (or lack thereof) of Harper's foreign-policy decision-making. Strategic thinking, not compassion, almost always motivates policy. One is hard-pressed to find an instance where compassion was more warranted than post-earthquake Haiti.

The internal files uncovered by the Canadian Press also confirm the government's antagonism towards Haiti's most popular political leader, Jean-Bertrand Aristide. On various occasions following Aristide's overthrow Ottawa expressed opposition to the former president's return from forced exile in South Africa, claiming in the words of ambassador Claude Boucher: "We consider Aristide a man of the past."

The Conservatives also actively supported or turned a blind eye to the exclusion of Aristide's Fanmi Lavalas, Haiti's most popular political party, from the 2009 senatorial and 2011 presidential elections. Just after the Canadian-financed 2009 poll Foreign Affairs spokeswoman Catherine Loubier congratulated Haiti's government for bringing "a period of stabilization" good for "investment and trade."

In late 2010/early-2011 the Conservatives helped extreme right-wing candidate Michel Martelly become president.

Canada put up $6 million for elections that excluded Lavalas from participating and following the first round of voting in November 2010 Canadian officials joined the international effort to force the candidate whom Haiti's electoral council had in second place, Jude Celestin, out of the runoff. After Martelly's supporters protested their candidate's third place showing, a six person Organization of American States (OAS) mission, including a Canadian representative, concluded that Martelly deserved to be in the second round. But, in analyzing the OAS methodology, the Washington-based Center for Economic and Policy Research, determined that "the Mission did not establish any legal, statistical, or other logical basis for its conclusions." Nevertheless, Ottawa and Washington pushed the Haitian government to accept the OAS's recommendations. Foreign minister Cannon said he "strongly urges the Provisional Electoral Council to accept and implement the [OAS] report's recommendations and to proceed with the next steps of the electoral process accordingly." In an interview he warned that "time is running out", adding that "our ambassador has raised this with the president [Rene Préval] himself." The Center for Economic and Policy Research described the intense western lobbying. "The international community, led by the US, France, and Canada, has been intensifying the pressure on the Haitian government to allow presidential candidate Michel Martelly to proceed to the second round of elections instead of [ruling party candidate] Jude Celestin." This pressure included some Haitian officials having their US visas revoked and there were threats that aid would be cut off if Martelly's vote total was not increased as per the OAS recommendation.

Half of Haiti's electoral council agreed to the OAS changes, but the other half did not. The second round was unconstitutional,

noted *Haïti Liberté*, as "only four of the eight-member Provisional Electoral Council (CEP) have voted to proceed with the second round, one short of the five necessary. Furthermore, the first round results have not been published in the journal of record, *Le Moniteur*, and President Préval has not officially convoked Haitians to vote, both constitutional requirements."

The absurdity of the whole affair did not stop the Canadian government from supporting the elections. Official election monitors from this country gave a thumbs-up to this exercise in what they said was democracy. After Martelly won the second round with 16.7 percent of registered voters support (with Lavalas boycotting only 22.8 percent of those eligible voted) Cannon declared: "We congratulate the people of Haiti, who exercised their fundamental democratic right to choose who will govern their country and represent them on the world stage." The left weekly *Haiti Progrès* took a different view. Describing the fraudulent nature of the elections, the paper explained: "The form of democracy that Washington, Paris and Ottawa want to impose on us is becoming a reality."

A supporter of the 1991 and 2004 coups against Aristide, Martelly was a teenaged member of the Duvalier dictatorship's Ton Ton Macoutes death squad. As president he has surrounded himself with former Duvalierists and death squad leaders. In January 2012 Martelly was quoted in the *New York Times* saying nobody wants Duvalier, who returned to Haiti after 25 years, prosecuted except for "certain institutions and governments" abroad.

Martelly's ties to Duvalierists didn't seem to bother John Baird. On a January 2012 trip to Haiti the foreign minister said he was pleased to see the "political will" to address the corruption and instability hampering Haiti's post-earthquake recovery. At the time

La Presse quoted Baird saying "[the Martelly administration] is going in the right direction." Of course, the Conservatives backed Martelly. Ottawa helped foster the political climate whereby this far right politician could win 'elections' even though he'd long shown disdain for the country's poor majority. Reporting on a stock of Wikileaks cables, *Haïti Liberté* described a December 1, 2009, meeting between the major foreign players in Haiti: "They were mostly worried about strengthening 'the opposition' (code for 'right-wing') which, for them, Préval had 'emasculated.' The EU and Canada therefore proposed that donors 'help level the playing field' by doing things like 'purchase radio air time for opposition politicians to plug their candidacies.' Otherwise, the right-wing 'will cease to be much of a meaningful force in the next government.'"

Of course, in the case of Haiti there is more than enough Canadian blame to go around. The Conservatives' policies towards Haiti were largely laid down by previous Liberal governments. In February 2004 Canada helped overthrow the country's elected government (Aristide and thousands of other elected officials). Paul Martin's government then provided important diplomatic, financial and military support to a brutal dictatorship that ruled for 27 months.

When Harper took office, according to a Wikileaks cable, the US ambassador in Ottawa asked the prime minister for "increasing [Canadian] support to the new government in Haiti, possibly even taking on more of a leadership role there." In the summer of 2006 the Conservatives entrenched the previous Liberal government's policy by announcing a five-year $550 million "aid" plan for Haiti. Harper further strengthened Canada's ties to the island nation when he visited Port-au-Prince in July 2007.

Some pro-democracy activists planned to oppose Harper's presence in Haiti. Leading Haitian human rights activist Pierre-Antoine Lovinsky, whom I met and worked with on a number of occasions, drafted a press release criticizing Canada's role in the country. (Exiled during the March 2004-May 2006 coup government, Lovinsky visited Ottawa and Montréal in March 2005 as part of a delegation to meet Liberal MP Denis Coderre, Paul Martin's special advisor on Haiti. At that time Lovinsky was quoted in the *Gazette* saying: "Canada is financing the oppression of Haiti, there's no other way to put it...The carnage has to stop.") A few hours before Harper's arrival in the slum neighbourhood of Cité Soleil many demonstrators were arrested. "On the morning of the 20th, our comrades went out into the streets with placards, banners, and megaphones," Lovinsky told *The Dominion* a few days later. "At that moment, it was around six in the morning, MINUSTAH [UN] soldiers began to make arrests for no reason. Many of our friends were arrested that morning."

Three weeks after Harper's visit Lovinsky, who was considering a run for Haiti's senate, disappeared after spending the day with an international solidarity mission. Three days later two members of the delegation, wrote Vancouver-based participant Roger Annis, "visited the Canadian embassy to urge Canadian ambassador Claude Boucher to make a public statement of concern about Lovinsky's disappearance. That request was refused by the embassy, and it has made no such statement to date." When someone of Lovinsky's profile goes missing in a country such as Iran or Venezuela Canadian officials often call for an investigation. But in Haiti, where they have a great deal of influence, Canada stayed quiet. The Haitian police never took Lovinsky's disappearance seriously and he has not been heard from since. In his report on

the delegation visit to the embassy, Canada Haiti Action Network coordinator Roger Annis noted that the second floor of the building was covered with pictures of Canadian police training their Haitian counterparts. Annis contrasted these photos with claims that there was nothing Canadian officials could do for Lovinsky, as if they had no influence over Haiti's police and judicial system.

A big chunk of Canada's aid to Haiti went towards a police and prison system that has been massively expanded and militarized since the February 2004 US/France/Canada coup. "We are going to help double the number of Haitian police trained," explained foreign minister Maxime Bernier in 2008.

Much to the delight of Haiti's über class-conscious elite, Ottawa took the lead in strengthening the repressive arm of the Haitian state. Moral implications be damned. In January 2009, for instance, Governor-General Michaëlle Jean presided over the opening of a Canadian-funded police station/jail in Torbeck. A week after the earthquake Haitian police, with UN "peacekeepers" in support, executed at least a dozen prisoners after an uprising/escape was thwarted at the Canadian built prison. (The vast majority of prisoners, it should be noted, had not been prosecuted and they apparently fled in fear of aftershocks.) More generally, the police regularly committed abuses. A 2011 investigation by the United Nation's Human Rights Office of the High Commissioner in Haiti found that police executions and torture were common.

Despite the crying need for housing and sanitation, after the earthquake the Conservatives ramped up spending on prisons and police. According to a report by Roger Annis, CIDA paid for 18 prisons to be built or refurbished and announced a total of $44 million in new security spending in the year after the quake. This $44 million was on top of $51 million put up for justice and security

system reform through Canada's Stabilization and Reconstruction Task Force, which began in 2006.

The Conservatives also strongly backed the militarization of Haiti. They ignored growing internal calls for an end to the UN occupation and instead pushed to extend the foreign military presence in Haiti. US State Department documents from late 2007 show that Canadian officials lobbied China, a veto-wielding member of the Security Council, to back a yearlong extension of the UN military mission. Unhappy about friendly relations between Haiti and Taiwan, Beijing preferred a six-month extension. The Chinese relented in the face of US and Canadian efforts. Similarly, in April 2009 Canada's representative at the UN argued there was "no alternative" to staying the course in Haiti. During the first UN General Assembly discussion on Haiti in three years, reported the *National Post*, Canadian officials called for the international force to remain as long as needed. Six months later foreign minister Cannon said: "Canada was pleased to co-sponsor the resolution to extend the mandate of the United Nations Stabilization Mission in Haiti, a priority mission for the international community that has enjoyed steady and significant progress." In November 2011 Ottawa gave $19 million to MINUSTAH (as the force is known in Haiti), which was one of many Canadian payments for the occupation force.

Among Haitians the UN force is highly controversial. By all accounts most of the country wants MINUSTAH to leave. There have been dozens of large protests against the UN military presence and a 2011 poll of Port au Prince residents found that most of the city had a negative opinion of the foreign troops. An August 2011 survey of over 800 households across Port-au-Prince by researchers from the Faculté d'Ethnologie de l'Université d'Etat

d'Haïti found that less than a quarter of respondents considered MINUSTAH's presence a "good thing" while 44 percent of respondents said UN agents are or have been engaged in criminal activities such as violence, theft and rape. Twenty one percent of those surveyed wanted MINUSTAH to leave Haiti "now" and another 22 percent of respondents wanted the troops to leave within a year. Only 5.9 percent of respondents said MINUSTAH should not leave Haiti. Outside of the capital, where there is less concern about personal security, opposition to MINUSTAH may even be stronger.

Since taking over from the US/French/Canadian troops that helped oust Aristide the UN force has been a tool of political repression. MINUSTAH backed up a violent political pacification campaign waged by the coup government's police force against poor neighbourhoods in Port-au-Prince from March 2004-May 2006. It also participated directly in attempts to pacify the slums, including a UN raid on July 6, 2005 that left dozens of civilians dead in Cité Soleil (a bastion of support for Aristide). In a January 15, 2007 interview with Haiti's Radio Solidarité Canada's ambassador, Claude Boucher, praised the UN troops for their violent raids, urging them to "increase their operations as they did last December." Boucher's public support for operations "last December" was an unmistakable reference to a December 22, 2006, UN assault on Cité Soleil. Dubbed the "Christmas Massacre" by neighbourhood residents, Agence France Presse indicated that at least 12 people were killed and "several dozen" wounded. Marketed by its architects as an action against "armed gangs" blamed for a spate of kidnappings, 400 troops, backed by helicopters, entered a densely populated residential area at 4:30 a.m. Eyewitnesses and victims of the attack claim MINUSTAH

helicopters fired on residents throughout the operation. The cardboard and corrugated tin wall houses were no match for the troops' heavy weaponry and the raid left scores of civilians dead and wounded, including women and children.

In April 2008 UN troops once again demonstrated that their primary purpose in the country was to defend the elite-dominated status quo. During riots over the rising cost of food they put down protests by killing demonstrators.

Aside from political repression UN troops have been accused of various abuses ranging from having sex with minors to sodomizing boys. Video footage came to light in January 2012 of five Uruguayan soldiers sexually assaulting an 18-year old Haitian. The soldiers were sent home but no one was punished. In February 2012 *Haïti Liberté* complained "there are also almost monthly cases of UN soldiers sexually assaulting Haitian minors, all of which have gone unpunished." According to the Status Forces Agreement signed between the UN and the coup government, MINUSTAH is not subject to Haitian laws. At worst, soldiers are sent home for trial. Despite committing countless crimes, this author is aware of only one MINUSTAH soldier being held to account at home.

In a bitter irony, UN soldiers from one of the poorest countries in Asia, Nepal, gave Haiti a disease that thrives in impoverished societies lacking adequate public sanitation and health systems. Ten months after the earthquake Nepalese troops brought a strain of cholera to Haiti that has left 7,000 dead and 700,000 ill. The October 2010 cholera outbreak began when excrement from soldiers at a base in Mirebalais was released into the Artibonite River. Despite conclusive evidence that the UN base was the source, MINUSTAH has refused to take responsibility.

Prominent French cholera expert Renaud Piarroux said the way in which the disease spread suggests there were "symptomatic cases" — soldiers with heavy diarrhea — on the base in Mirebalais. In other words, some officials at the UN base would have at least suspected that soldiers carried the disease yet the sewage from the base continued to be dumped into a stream from which people drank and bathed.

Ten months after their reckless sewage disposal caused the cholera outbreak UN forces displayed a similar disregard for Haitian health. On two occasions in August 2011 UN trucks were caught dumping feces and other waste in holes near water streams where people bathed and drank.

After the January 12, 2010, earthquake five billion dollars was pledged to reconstruct Haiti. Most of the money that was distributed went to foreign aid workers who received relatively extravagant salaries/living costs or to expensive contracts gobbled up by Western/Haitian elite owned companies. As this book went to print, two and a half years after the earthquake, the situation remained dire. About 400,000 Haitians still lived in refugee camps and only 5,000 permanent homes had been built.

Unfortunately, this was all too predictable. Asked my thoughts on Canada's role in Haiti the day after the quake, I told *Globe and Mail* reporter Paul Koring that so long as the power dynamics in the country did not shift there would be little change. "'Cynically, it feels like a 'pity time for the Haitians' but I doubt much will really change,' says Yves Engler, a left-wing activist from Montreal who blames the United States, along with Canada, for decades of self-interested meddling in Haitian affairs. 'We bear some responsibility ... because our policies have undermined Haiti's capacity to deal with natural disasters,' he said."

As we've seen the Conservatives' immediate concern was dominating, not helping, Haiti. Similarly, Washington and the tiny Haitian ruling class did not change their ways after the earthquake. Thirteen days after the quake the Conservatives organized a high profile Ministerial Preparatory Conference on Haiti for major international donors. Two months later Canada co-chaired the New York International Donors' Conference Towards a New Future for Haiti. At these conferences Haitian officials played a tertiary role in the discussions.

In the months after the quake the major powers in Haiti – led by the US, France and Canada – demanded the Haitian parliament pass an 18-month long state of emergency law that effectively gave up government control over the reconstruction. They held up money to ensure international control of the Interim Commission for the Reconstruction of Haiti, authorized to spend billions in reconstruction money.

The only way for Haiti to move forward is to build that country's capacity to run its own affairs. But that requires some level of democracy and Harper's Conservatives do not trust ordinary people to run their own affairs. Certainly not Haitians, probably not Canadians either.

11. Conclusion

As shown in the case studies above, the Harper
government shifted Canadian foreign policy from the mainstream
to the extreme right among the leading capitalist countries. The
obvious first question is why. As this author's previous works have
demonstrated, Canada has long taken a pro-corporate/pro-empire
approach to foreign policy. But, some nominal "independence"
from the dominant powers was often valued so this country could
at least pretend to be an "honest broker" in mediating disputes. (In
his memoir former prime minister Jean Chrétien recounts telling
president Bill Clinton, "Keeping some distance will be good for
both of us. If we look as though we're the fifty-first state of the
United States, there's nothing we can do for you internationally, just
as the governor of a state can't do anything for you internationally.
But if we look independent enough, we can do things for you that
even the CIA cannot do.") That centrist pretence has been entirely
abandoned by the Harper Conservatives and replaced with a
foreign policy that occupies the far right of the political spectrum.

There are electoral, ideological and structural reasons
for this shift. Harper's foreign policy has been designed to please
the most reactionary, short sighted sectors of the party's base —
the ideological right, evangelical Christians, right-wing Zionists,
Islamophobes, old Cold-Warriors, the military-industrial-complex
as well as mining and oil executives.

Foreign policy has been used as a wedge issue to win
votes from particular ethnic or religious interest groups. One aim
of the Foreign Affairs' Office of Religious Freedom was to woo
right-wing religious groups. In March 2012 Postmedia reported on

internal files showing Baird and his political staff closely vetting a controversial list of invitees to the Office of Religious Freedom's inaugural meeting. "The invitation list prompted criticism because it included religious communities with significant influence in key ridings as well as a large number of Judeo-Christian groups that have been friendly to the Conservative government while excluding many others." No Sunni or Shia Muslim leader was invited. Nor were any representatives from the Buddhist, Sikh and Hindu faiths. Panellists included a prominent evangelical Christian, a Catholic priest, the head of the Jewish group B'nai Brith and a Baha'i community leader.

Representatives from more left-leaning Christian groups were also excluded. The Conservatives were hostile to Christian groups such as Kairos, an ecumenical organization representing 11 churches, and, as outlined above, even cut its CIDA aid funding. While criticism of Israel was the reason given for the cut, this was only one of many issues that separated Kairos from more right-leaning Christian organizations. As Marci Macdonald details in the *Armageddon Factor* the Conservatives are closest to the fundamentalist evangelical organizations and Harper himself is a member of the Christian and Missionary Alliance church.

Much has been made of Harper's attempt to lure Jewish voters and donors from the Liberals by supporting Israel's aggressive policies. This strategy has had some success, but at just over 1% of the population the Jewish community is far too small to fully explain the Conservatives' position. Rather than Jewish votes Harper's 'Israel no matter what' policy had more to do with mobilizing his right wing, evangelical base on an issue (unlike abortion) with limited electoral downside. Since the 9/11 terrorist attacks in the US, Israel's supporters have aggressively promoted

the idea that Israel is on the front line of the West's fight against the all-encompassing boogeyman known as Islamic terrorism. In a CBC interview on the tenth anniversary of the 9/11 attacks Harper called "Islamic terrorism" the biggest security threat to Canada. "When people think of Islamic terrorism, they think of Afghanistan, or maybe they think of some place in the Middle East, but the truth is that threat exists all over the world." The Secretary-General of the 57-member Organization of Islamic Cooperation, Ekmeleddin Ihsanoglu, responded by saying "Harper's statement will only exacerbate the misunderstanding and suspicion between the West and the Islamic world and obstruct global efforts to confront bigotry and hatred between religions and cultures."

While it was likely insulting to the one billion people represented by the Organization of Islamic Cooperation, Harper's comment certainly played well with staunchly anti-Islamic sectors of the Conservative party such as Charles McVety's organization. And if polls are to be believed, broad swaths of the public would not disagree with Harper's attitude. According to an early 2012 survey of 1,522 Canadians conducted by Leger Marketing, 52 percent of Canadians don't trust Muslims.

Harper's Islamophobic comments were designed to stoke an 'us-and-them' sentiment. In July 2011 the prime minister told *Maclean's* that global politics is a "struggle between good and bad". Presumably, Harper wants his electoral base to see him as a leader of the Judeo-Christian alliance waging this apocalyptic struggle.

Harper's right wing religious/nationalist storyline seemed to mimic US president George Bush's 'war on terror' initiative, which also engendered an 'us-and-them' sentiment all the while promoting militarism. On the tenth anniversary of the

twin towers terrorist attack the Conservatives made September 11 National Day of Service to "pay tribute to the victims and their loved ones, [and] we also honour members of the military, law enforcement and intelligence personnel who continue to fight on the front lines against all forms of terrorism." It may seem odd for a Canadian government to devote a day to the "men in uniform" tied to 2,800 (mostly) office workers dying in New York, but for the Conservatives it was an opportunity to focus attention on their support for generally popular military and security officials. As a general rule, the Conservatives benefit by directing public discussion towards national security and militarism (as opposed to issues such as healthcare and daycare).

On the day the navy's National Shipbuilding Procurement Strategy was signed Harper presided over ceremonial events on both the west and east coasts. In the morning the prime minister signed the accord with Irving Shipbuilding in Halifax and then flew across the country to do the same with Seaspan in BC. The aim was to maximize media attention in both the Maritimes and BC as well as nationally. The $33 billion National Shipbuilding Procurement Strategy benefits the Conservatives by boosting its corporate friends' profits, creating some well-paying jobs and enhancing its military credentials, which are an important part of its patriotic brand.

In a March 2012 interview with Québec magazine *l'Actualité* Harper's former chief of staff and long-time advisor Tom Flanagan explained how right wing governments need to foster patriotism to be successful. "Everywhere in the world conservative parties rarely win elections if they are not recognized as the party of patriotism," he said. This is another way of saying that governments completely suppliant to big business must

provide the working class majority with a reason to vote against their own material interests.

Of course, there have been various facets to the Conservatives' patriotic brand. One element has been to promote Canada's British colonial heritage. The Conservatives have repeatedly celebrated the royal family, funded monarchist groups and returned to the pre-1968 titles Royal Canadian Navy and Royal Canadian Air Force. *Warrior Nation* explains: "The application of 'royal' to institutions left and right may seem comical, but one would be ill-advised to minimize the extent to which the British sovereign is a deeply meaningful symbol of whiteness, hierarchy and authoritarian rule." Another way they have developed their patriotic brand has been to associate themselves with 'Canadian' sports. Harper regularly attends high-profile hockey and curling matches. All this fits with the Conservatives claim to be defending 'Western civilization' both ideologically as well as militarily.

From Afghanistan to Libya, militarism has been a big part of their patriotic brand. At times they have focused on Arctic sovereignty to generate a sense of militarized patriotism. Privately, US officials dismissed the Conservatives' Arctic announcements as having little to do with enforcing sovereignty in the North and instead designed to attract votes. "Conservatives make concern for 'The North' part of their political brand and it works," noted a January 2010 cable from the US Embassy in Ottawa released by WikiLeaks.

Beyond electoral and ideological considerations, powerful economic forces have driven the Conservatives' extreme foreign policy. While the post 9-11 'war on terror' climate led to a wave of anti-Islam sentiment exploited by the Conservatives, it also led to a rise of militarism, which has been good for groups such as the

Canadian Association of Defence and Security Industries as well as many within the shipping, aerospace and high-tech industries.

Over the past two decades the Canadian corporate class has become increasingly transnational and dependent on neoliberal capitalist reforms (privatization of state owned assets, a retrenchment in social entitlements and the liberalization of international investment rules). Montréal-based SNC-Lavalin, for instance, benefited from governments around the world shifting to public-private partnerships. One of the world's biggest engineering firms, the company has projects in 100 countries. In a similar fashion, the privatization of war served GardaWorld, which grew to 45,000 employees. This Montréal-based company did significant business in Iraq and Afghanistan and in mid-2012 lobbied the Transportation Security Administration to privatize US airport security.

Corporate Canada's most powerful sector has also quietly benefited from neoliberal globalization. The liberalization of global banking regulations benefited Canadian banks, which rank among the largest in the world. Scotiabank, for example, operates in 45 countries and most of the big five banks now do more business outside of Canada than in. The Canadian mining industry has benefited from neoliberal reforms such as the privatization of state-run mining companies, loosening restrictions on foreign investment and reductions in government royalty rates. Over the past two decades Canadian mining investment has exploded. Canadian mining assets in Africa grew 80 fold between 1989 and 2011 from $250 million to over $20 billion. The situation is similar in many Latin American countries. For instance, there were no Canadian mines operating in Mexico in 1994. By 2010 there were about 375 Canadian-run projects. Before the reforms

that came with the North American Free Trade Agreement, Mexico's constitution dictated that land, subsoil and its riches were the property of the state and recognized the collective right of communities to land through the *ejido* system. Constitutional changes in 1992 allowed for sale of lands to third parties, including multinational corporations. Combined with a new Law on Foreign Investment, the Mining Law of 1992 allowed for 100 percent foreign control in the exploration and production of mines. With hundreds of projects in Mexico, Canadian mining companies have been the biggest winners from these reforms.

Any government that increases resource royalty rates or nationalizes extractive industries is a threat to Canadian mining interests. Yet, these types of reforms are often the first pushed by governments and social movements resisting neoliberalism. A July 2012 *Globe and Mail* business headline described the phenomenon this way: "In Latin America, nationalism stumps Canadian [resource] companies" while that same month an *Embassy* headline noted: "Canadian mining firms confront new wave of Latin American nationalization." Put simply, Canadian mining profits are closely tied to maintaining, if not expanding, extreme free market capitalism. This reality has pushed Ottawa towards a more aggressive international posture.

Canada's growing 'petro state' status has also driven a more extreme, anti-internationalist, foreign policy. Tar sands growth basically guarantees that Canada will oppose or flout international agreements to reduce greenhouse gas emissions. Peter Kent made this point forcefully in March 2012 when he described the Kyoto Protocol as "probably the biggest foreign policy mistake the previous Liberal government made." The politicians most committed to tar sands expansion have an

incentive to build hostility towards international accords and the UN. This is an important point that needs to be explored further. Did the Conservatives constant criticism of the UN's 'bias' against Israel undermine the organization's credibility in the eyes of some? This and other Conservative attacks against the international organization likely weakened support for UN-sponsored climate negotiations, a benefit to tar sands interests.

Whatever the reasons for the Conservatives' shift to the right, those of us who want Canada to adopt a more just foreign policy are up against powerful systemic forces and an ideologically driven government. But these obstacles aren't insurmountable. The vast majority of Canadians didn't vote for Harper's Conservatives and many aren't happy with the new reality of an "Ugly Canadian" foreign policy. Most don't want Canada to be disliked on the international stage. Nor do most Canadians want Ottawa to further impoverish the Global South.

So how do we get from Harper's foreign policy to one that more closely represents the majority of Canadians' attitudes and interests? The only way to do so is to mobilize grassroots people power, which is not easy to do when foreign affairs decisions are far removed from most Canadians day-to-day lives.

First off, it's vital to make foreign policy a major topic of discussion in the lead-up to the next election. But, we can't wait for the opposition parties to do all the work. Grassroots groups must force the issue if we expect any sustained discussion in the House of Commons or on the campaign trail. All those working for peace, in solidarity with Palestine and Haiti as well as those challenging destructive Canadian mining practices and the government's abominable environmental record, should make common cause. We need to work together.

We need to build a multi-issue alliance that forthrightly challenges Harper's destructive foreign policy. Individually, the groups working on these campaigns aren't strong enough to have a significant impact. Together it might be a different story. The combined energy, creativity and resources could ignite a movement that is more powerful than the sum of its parts. It may even tip the scales in favour of ecological and social justice.

No multi-issue network is possible if we ghettoize our campaigns. It is imperative to highlight how issues are connected. No one doubts that those challenging the Conservatives' support for mining interests abroad and for tar sands producers are fighting against a similar corporate mentality, but it may be less obvious what groups fighting for Palestinian rights and the environment have in common. The answer is that in addition to having a common foe, both Palestine solidarity and climate justice groups would win a substantial victory if the Conservatives were forced to follow the established UN consensus. More generally, the Conservatives' position on these two issues reflects deference to power no matter the social consequences.

One way to build such a cross issue alliance is to highlight how a specific misdeed fits the pattern of the Conservatives pro-corporate/pro-empire foreign policy. Too often, groups try to isolate their critique by claiming Canada is a force for good except for the one particular immoral position being criticized.

One proposal could be that a multi-issue network be established with a countrywide popular education campaign to "Stop Harper's Crimes Against Humanity." As part of that campaign stickers could be produced with the above slogan and bullet points touching on climate change, mining, Palestinian rights and militarism. T-shirts with a picture of Harper and the

slogan "Wanted: for crimes against humanity" could be sold to raise money for the stickers. The stickers and t-shirts could direct people to a website with information on the issues. Part of the goal of the first phase of a campaign might be to build a coalition of the various organizations already working on these issues.

If the campaign gains traction, a popular tribunal with high profile judges to investigate Harper's crimes against humanity could be organized. One medium-term goal of a cross-issue network could be to target five or six ridings where Conservative MPs are vulnerable. This is an entirely achievable goal.

During the 2006 election the author of this book and others participated in a campaign to defeat foreign minister Pierre Pettigrew because of his role in overthrowing the elected government of Haiti. A dozen of us handed out 15,000 leaflets and put up 2,000 posters with his photo and the tag line "Wanted: for crimes against humanity in Haiti". We also organized a series of rallies and press conferences in his riding, where about 4,000 members of the Haitian diaspora were living. Both *La Presse* and *Le Devoir* noted that our campaign contributed to the foreign minister's narrow defeat. Even before Pettigrew lost we considered our efforts a success as the campaign generated significant media attention about Canada's destructive role in Haiti. Many elements of the Pettigrew campaign could be repeated elsewhere.

When criticizing Harper's foreign policy let's be forthright. If we want people to take the time to investigate issues that are distant from their daily affairs it's particularly important to convey the gravity of the situation. We should be clear that foreign military interventions kill and that the Conservatives' climate policy is devastating many of the world's most vulnerable. Let the opposition parties soften the language or package the information

in a politically palatable way. Our goal should be to force open the narrow parameters of foreign-policy debate. To move beyond what Noam Chomsky calls "the bounds of the expressible." We absolutely need to shake Canadians from their complacency. Many people oppose the Conservatives' bid to undermine international climate negotiations and are uncomfortable with their unflinching support for Israeli policy. It's time to turn that discomfort into anger and the anger into action. Please join a group working on these issues. The world needs your help.

Acknowledgements

I would like to thank Jennifer Moore from Mining Watch and Roger Annis with the Canada Haiti Action Network for editing chapters. I would also like to acknowledge my mother Bernadette Stringer and uncle Al Engler's help in looking over the manuscript. Similarly, I'd like to thank Bianca Mugyenyi for her support and the use of parts of our book *Stop Signs: Cars and Capitalism on the Road to Economic, Social and Ecological Decay*. Finally, I'd like to thank my father, Gary Engler, for editing the manuscript.

Resources for Activists

Organizations

Anti-war
Canadian Peace Alliance (many cities)
Coalition to Oppose the Arms Trade (Ottawa)
Project Ploughshares (Waterloo)
Science for Peace (Toronto)

Mining Justice
Mining Watch (Ottawa)
Mining Injustice Solidarity Network (Toronto)
Rights Action (Toronto)
Protest Barrick (Toronto)
Canadians Against Mining Injustices in Peru

Green Groups
Climate Action Network Canada
Climate Justice (many cities)
Canadian Youth Climate Coalition
Green Action Centre (Winnipeg)
Greenpeace

Palestine
Canadians for Justice and Peace in the Middle East (many cities)
Solidarity for Palestinian Human Rights (many campus chapters)
Coalition Against Israeli Apartheid (many cities)
Independent Jewish Voices - Canada (many cities)
Students Against Israeli Apartheid (various campus chapters)
Tadamon! (Montreal)
Canada Palestine Association (Vancouver)

Resources for Activists (continued)

Latin America solidarity

Canada Haiti Action Network (many cities)
Common Frontiers (Toronto)
Colombia Action Solidarity Alliance (Toronto)
Committee for Human Rights in Latin America (Montréal)
Latin American and Caribbean Solidarity Network (Toronto)
Latin American Trade Unionists Coalition (Ontario)
Maritimes-Guatemala Breaking the Silence Network
The Project for Accompaniment and Solidarity with Colombia
(Montréal)
Toronto Bolivia Solidarity
Latin American Canadian Solidarity Association (London)
Reseau Quebecois sur l'integration Continentale

Africa/Asia solidarity

Groupe de Recherche et d'Initiative pour la Libération de
l'Afrique (Montreal)
Network for Pan-Afrikan Solidarity (Toronto)
Solidarity Committee for Ethiopian Political Prisoners (Canada)
Canada-Philippines Solidarity for Human Rights